Bookbinding

BOOKBINDING

A MANUAL OF TECHNIQUES

Pamela Richmond

The Crowood Press

First published in 1989 by
The Crowood Press
Ramsbury, Marlborough
Wiltshire SN8 2HE

British Library Cataloguing in Publication Data

Richmond, Pamela
  Bookbinding: a manual of techniques
  1. Hand bookbinding. Manuals
  I. Title
  686.3'02

  ISBN 1 85223 175 0

Acknowledgements

With thanks to my mother and father, and to
Daphne Beaumont-Wright for her help with the
first part of the book.

Picture credits

Line illustrations by Sharon Perks
Photographs by Martin Griffiths

Typeset by Inforum Typesetting, Portsmouth
Printed in Great Britain by The Bath Press

Contents

Introduction

'Bookbinder', announced a visitor to my workshop, gazing at me curiously. 'You don't see them any more.' But I don't feel like an endangered species and certainly the people I teach seem to be under no threat of extinction. It is for these keen amateur binders that this book has been written, with detailed notes that will offer an introduction to bookbinding through cloth work. These notes are based on the work done by these amateur binders who, despite limited and frequently inadequate equipment, constantly surprise and delight me with their work, enthusiasm and resourcefulness.

Many of the projects can be done at home with a minimum of equipment and I hope that the notes can be followed by an average evening class student. They are not intended, however, to be a sole means of instruction – nothing can replace a good teacher explaining and, most important of all, demonstrating.

The chapter on repairs deals with the sort of problems encountered most commonly by students. I must stress that repairs should only be attempted after basic bookbinding principles have been thoroughly mastered, and even then to start with you should work only on old friends that have succumbed to use and age in order to render them whole and readable again.

I have learned much while writing this book – not least that there is always more than one way of doing almost anything, but most of all that it is far more enjoyable to *do* bookbinding than to write about it!

1 Where to Work

If you were to visit a bindery with no previous knowledge of bookbinding, you might be forgiven for wondering exactly what went on there, as there would be a bewildering array of devices for pressing, heating, holding and cutting. The prospect of setting up a home workshop can seem rather daunting, but it is possible to do some binding at home without any particularly heavy equipment. As you progress you will find that there is no substitute for well-made tools that are specially designed for the job, but, having said that, I never advise students to rush out and buy expensive tools. Much can be achieved in the beginning with basic hand tools while working on a clean, firm table. However, once you find that you have become addicted to bookbinding, a room of your own in which to work will become desirable.

YOUR WORKSHOP

Your workshop need not be large – mine is 12 × 10ft (about 3.5 × 3m) – but it should have a good supply of natural daylight and be dry, as any dampness will cause materials to warp. For convenience a ground-floor situation is preferable, but not essential.

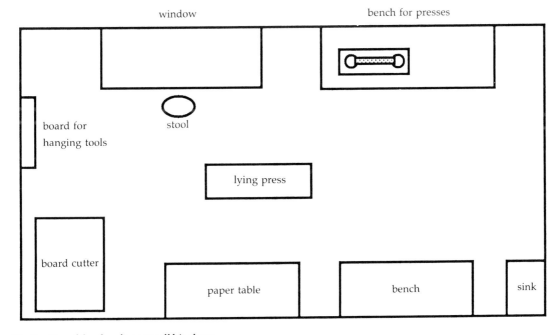

Fig 1 Possible plan for a small bindery.

Electricity and Lighting

A good supply of natural light is invaluable – it is the best light of all to work by – but some form of artificial light will still be needed. Although fluorescent strips are convenient and economical, they do not give as true a light for working as strategically-placed spot lights or, for more detailed work, an angle-poise lamp.

You will always need more power points than you think. If you can afford the luxury of starting from scratch, and having a truly 'fitted' workshop, then two power points placed above one bench on the wall will save much grovelling about in dingy corners. At least another two points, again conveniently placed but perhaps this time at a lower level, will prove useful.

Heating

Although your workshop should not be damp, an atmosphere that is too dry or hot is equally undesirable, as this too can cause damage to materials. For those of you who are interested in statistics, the ideal climate for storing books and related materials is between 55°F and 65° (13–18°C), with a relative humidity of 55–65 per cent (from *Caring for Books and Documents*, A D Baynes-Cope). Bear these figures in mind, particularly if you have central heating or storage heaters in winter. If additional heating is required while you are working either a small electric or gas heater is suitable, although do remember if you are working in a small enclosed space that when gas burns water is formed. If you have no central heating a low-voltage electric heater which can be left on all the time will keep the temperature in your room steady.

Water

Easy access to water is necessary. A small sink in a corner of your workshop is most desirable, but for the amateur binder working at home this is not absolutely vital.

Furniture

Benches

Your main working area could be a stout table, but this could take up valuable space, and as bookbinding is often carried out standing up, could prove to be at an uncomfortable height. A good working height for your bench is 3–3ft 3in (90–97.5cm), although this will obviously depend upon the height and build of the binder. If you are building your own bench, a good indication is that your hands with elbows bent should lie comfortably and naturally on the working surface. The depth of the bench should be 2ft 6in–3ft (75–90cm), and the minimum length is 6ft (180cm) – you will find that you easily use up all available space, however much there is! A second bench that is slightly lower in height is a useful addition.

If you are making your own bench, it should be as sturdy as possible with storage space underneath. It is also a good idea to have a little 'fence' about 1in (2.5cm) high along the back and short sides of your bench, to prevent small items vanishing. The surface of your bench should be as smooth and easy to keep clean as possible – plastic-coated chipboard screwed in place is very suitable for this purpose, and this is available from most timber merchants who will cut it to the length you require.

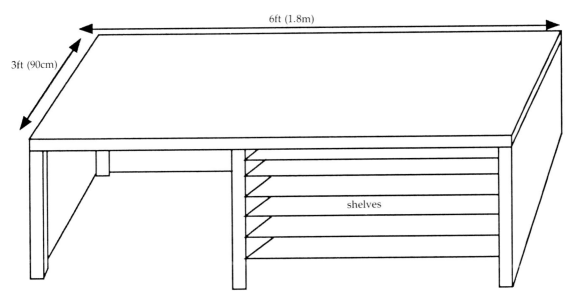

Fig 2   The work bench.

A particularly strong bench for holding a nipping press is essential. Nipping presses are heavy and should be positioned over a supporting leg, and they should also be bolted to the bench for safety as they tend to 'walk'. A rather obvious point to consider (but easily overlooked) is to place your press with sufficient room behind to allow the arms to pass through 360°.

If you do not have a carpenter in the family perfectly adequate and fairly strong benches can be made from old kitchen units found in junk shops. These often have useful cupboards, drawers and shelves and are usually made at a good working height. I have made a long bench using two such units with a sheet of plastic (melamine) coated board as the working surface.

Another source of useful and interesting bindery furniture is shops that are closing down or refurbishing. These are often willing to give, or sell cheaply, counters, desks and shelf units, again offering interesting and useful storage space as well as a firm working surface.

Paper Table

Storing paper can be a problem. It must be kept flat, dry and clean and yet be easily accessible – nothing is more frustrating than trying to ease one sheet of paper from a heap of fifty or more different sheets. A paper table can quite easily be made beneath one of your benches. Mine is under the bench holding the nipping presses as I don't actually work on that bench, and so the paper has less chance of being soiled or trampled on. The shelf size must be deep and wide enough to take your largest sheet of paper, ideally 40in (100cm) wide by 36in (90cm) deep, but at least 36in by 36in (90 × 90cm). The shelves are placed on wooden runners made from 1 × 1in (2.5 × 2.5cm) battens of wood nailed to the inside legs or walls of your bench. Note that if you are making your paper table from an actual table the two

11

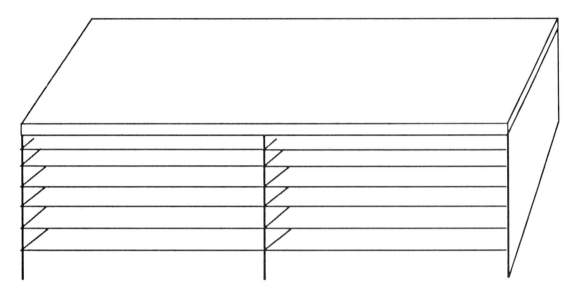

Fig 3   The paper table.

Fig 4   Part of the author's bindery, showing the tool board, presses, paper table and lying press.

outer sides and the back should be enclosed. Your shelves should be 4–5in (10–12.5cm) apart, enabling you to fit seven or eight shelves in, and thus keep different papers separately, with the sliding shelves facilitating access.

Seating

Although much of your work will be accomplished standing, you will find that a tall stool (about 28in (70cm) high) is useful.

2 Tools and Equipment

BASIC EQUIPMENT

You will probably find that you already have many of this first group of tools and they just need gathering together.

- Pencils – H and HB. These should always be sharp, as you will be dealing with small measurements and a thick line will lead to inaccuracies.
- Rubber
- 45° set square – preferably plastic and with pointed rather than rounded corners
- L square/carpenter's square – a metal one is preferable, the most useful length being 7in (17.5cm)
- Pair of size 8 knitting needles
- Toothbrush
- Tweezers
- A selection of sand papers – glass paper, emery paper

Essential Small Hand Tools

Most of these tools can be bought from either a good ironmonger or an art shop. Always buy the best you can afford as your tools should last you many years and will become old friends – although it is a bad craftsman who blames his tools, poor quality ones will not make life easier. It is sometimes possible to buy good second-hand tools from specialist art shops.

Spring Dividers

These can be set to a certain measurement and are invaluable. Ordinary school dividers will not do, as they cannot be set and are too inaccurate. Spring dividers come in many sizes, from tiny ones with a span of $3\frac{1}{2}$in (8.75cm) to very large ones spanning 14in (35cm) or more. I suggest that you start with a pair with a span of about 7in (17.8cm) and then add to your collection with a smaller and a larger pair as necessary. These can be obtained from good ironmongers and tool shops. If you buy an old pair, do check that the thread of the screw is not worn and that the points are sharp, as you will be dealing with small, accurate measurements.

Metal Ruler

This should be a 12in (30cm) metal ruler, marked in imperial and metric. The inches should be divided into $\frac{1}{16}$. It should be guaranteed rustless.

Metal Straight Edge

Although not essential at first, a heavy longer metal straight edge of 24–36in (60–90cm) is very useful. This and the ruler can be bought from ironmongers.

Scissors or Shears

Bookbinding shears are large, heavy-duty scissors, and to facilitate cutting the top

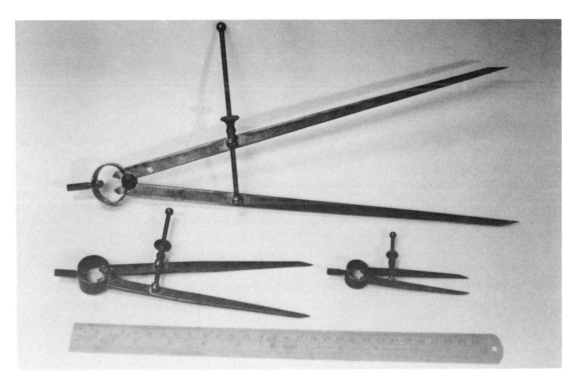

Fig 5   Some of the bookbinder's hand tools – (top) pointed bone folder, small brush, needle and L-square or carpenter's square; (bottom) metal ruler, small, medium and large dividers.

blade is blunt, instead of ending in a point. These seem to be obtainable only from bookbinding suppliers or second-hand tool shops. A pair of large, good quality scissors will do, although they will not last as long. A pair of small sharp scissors for trimming threads and tapes is always useful.

Scalpel

A surgeon's scalpel is a very useful acquisition. A No. 3 Swann-Morton handle will take No. 10, 10a, and 12 blades, and all can be bought from a good chemist or an art or model shop. The advantage of a scalpel is that you can always have a sharp clean blade for trimming. The three different numbers I have mentioned apply to three different types of blade – 10 is the most useful, for trimming and cutting, and also (when blunt) for lifting paper or cloth from board. A No. 12 blade is very useful for undoing sewing – the blade is curved, so the chances of damaging the paper are lessened – and the No. 10a is useful for trimming small difficult areas. If you only want to invest in one type of blade, the No. 10 is your best bet.

An addition to the scalpel is a craft knife with replaceable blades. Again you have the advantage of a readily-available sharp new blade, but once the blade is blunt and replaced it cannot be re-used. I have found that with the smaller knives the side screw can get in the way and make a straight and accurate cut difficult.

Bone Folder

The bone folder is perhaps the most indispensable tool, and in time seems to become an extension of your hand. They are available in several lengths, from 4in to 8in (10–20cm). I prefer working with a smaller one, but people do differ. Folders are slightly curved and either have one pointed and one rounded end or two rounded ends. You may find that the point of your new bone folder benefits from a little smoothing and thinning down with coarse and then fine sandpaper. They are available from good art and craft shops and specialist suppliers.

Brushes

You will find a selection of brushes useful – a small water-colour brush, No. 2, and two flat-headed nylon brushes $\frac{1}{4}$in and $\frac{1}{2}$in (0.5cm and 1cm) wide. I have found that the best brushes for pasting and glueing are pure bristle archivist brushes, available from bookbinding suppliers, although to start with two $\frac{1}{2}$in (1cm) paint brushes (one for glue and one for paste) will do.

Needles

Needles for bookbinding are necessarily strong with a fairly round eye. They are obtainable from bookbinding suppliers in various sizes – No. 18 will suffice for most jobs, although a finer one for slender volumes will be useful. Ordinary sewing needles tend to be too fine or weak for bookbinding, and embroidery needles too coarse. Darning needles have been used by students with some success, although they lack the sturdiness of the real thing.

Saw

A small tenon saw with very fine teeth can be used, although a hack-saw blade attached to a wooden handle is just as useful.

Hammer

Your backing hammer should be kept as clean and smooth as possible – it is not for knocking in nails. It differs from a carpenter's hammer by its head which has one smooth, slightly rounded face, and one wedged-shaped face, or peen, again with a slightly curved surface. Different weights of hammer are available, and it is advisable to use as heavy a one as you comfortably can handle.

Knocking Down Iron

This is a flat piece of iron, about $8 \times 4 \times \frac{1}{2}$ in ($20 \times 10 \times 1$cm), with a solid central bar or handle. As with your hammer the surface of this should be kept as smooth and clean as possible. It is used in cloth work for hammering out the joints in book sections and for knocking out the swell, and it can also be used as a weight. Although actual knocking down irons are only obtainable through specialist suppliers, it should be possible to have one made by a metalworker or blacksmith.

Weights

It seems as though, like power points, you can never have too many weights. Old flat irons, old-fashioned weights and even odd lumps of metal weighing between $\frac{1}{4}$lb and 8lb (100g and 3.5kg) are all of use. Naturally they should be as rust-free and smooth-faced as possible to avoid accidental damage to books or material. A large flat iron can act as a substitute knocking down iron.

Boards

Pressing Boards

Your local wood merchant should be able to provide you with pressing boards if you ask for $\frac{3}{8}$–$\frac{5}{8}$ plywood, and most will also cut the boards to size for you. It is a good idea to have several pairs of different-sized pressing boards, and at least two pairs of each size – 12 × 18in (30 × 45cm), 9 × 12in (22.5 × 30cm) and 9 × 6in (22.5 × 15cm), for example.

If you can cover your boards with melamine they will be easy to clean and you can be certain they will not damage your work.

Backing Boards

These are wedge-shaped pieces of hard wood, usually beech, with the wider edge planed off to 60°. Again, it is advisable to have various lengths to cope with different sizes of book, but if you only want to buy one pair to begin with, a pair of 15in (37.5cm) boards is suitable for most books. A longer and a shorter pair can be added later.

Metal Plates

Often known as tin plates, these are usually made of a rust-free metal such as aluminium or zinc. It is best to get four sheets cut of each size to fit your pressing boards. Both plates and pressing boards should be kept scratch-free and as clean as possible, because any slight scratch mark will undoubtedly transfer itself to the book or paper being pressed.

Fig 6   Pair of backing boards and backing hammer.

LARGE EQUIPMENT

Laying or Lying Press

This is perhaps the single most useful piece of equipment. It is used for many different operations, from simply holding the book for cleaning off or glueing, to rounding and backing, to trimming. It can also be used as a finishing press and even as a substitute nipping press for smaller books.

The press consists of two wooden cheeks, made of well-seasoned beech. In this case there are two metal screws – traditionally wooden screws were used, but, although wooden screws can be kinder, metal screws are perfectly adequate and have the advantage that they are less vulnerable to damage. They are also easier to produce and obtain and thus help to keep down the cost. The cheeks

should be solid, 40 × 5 × 5in (100 × 12.5 × 12.5cm), with at least 28in (70cm) between the screws. There are also two wooden guide bars which help to keep the cheeks of the press straight and avoid any twisting which could occur.

The press sits in a stand called a tub. Again, this should be sturdily made, and a comfortable working height when the press is in position is 34–36in (85–90cm). The tub should be wide enough to accommodate the fully-opened press. The legs of the tub are angled slightly inwards, as the binder works mainly from the end of the press, and this angling allows you to get closer to the book by providing a foot place.

If the press is turned on to its side it can then be used as a nipping press.

Turn the press right over and you have the ploughing side. On one of the cheeks are two parallel strips of wood forming a

Fig 7   The tub for the lying press.

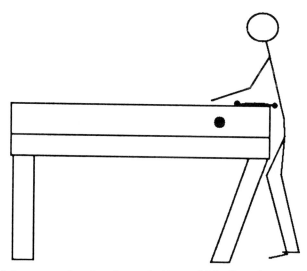

Fig 8   The tub for the lying press, showing the angled legs which allow the binder to stand as close as possible to the work.

Fig 9   The lying press in its tub.

track for the plough. Although great care should be taken at all times to protect the press, the ploughing side should be used for ploughing only, as an absolutely smooth surface is essential.

The press screws are tightened with the help of a metal bar which slots through a hole in the screw handles. When you are tightening the screws it is essential that you do it evenly and equally, as unequal pressure on your book will not only result in an oddly-shaped and possibly damaged book, but could also hurt your press. Check that they are even by measuring the distance between the screws, with dividers held flat so that the points are touching the exact inside edges of the cheeks.

Lying presses are not cheap. They can be bought from specialist suppliers or direct from the makers, some of whom have been developing exciting new designs for central screw and multi-functional presses. Lying presses can also be bought second-hand, again from suppliers or occasionally from binderies or printing works that are closing down. Although it is nice to have old tools and equipment, do check the press thoroughly for woodworm and other beasts. Also, ensure that the cheeks of the press have not been badly hammered and that it is possible to plane them smooth, that the cheeks have not bowed or become distorted in any way, and that the screws are not chipped or broken.

20

Fig 10   The ploughing side of the lying press, showing plough tracks.

Fig 11   The plough.

21

Presses made for hobbyists are available but they are usually small and rather insubstantial, and are really not strong enough for the job. Although they are less expensive than a proper press, it is a false economy.

Plough

A plough consists of two parallel wooden cheeks connected by two guide bars and a central wooden screw with handle. The blade is held on the underside by a metal holder, with three angled jaws to prevent the blade from falling out. The two outer jaws are rigid while the middle one is attached to a screw. The blade is slid in place from the side and held by tightening the wing nut.

Finishing Press

Finishing is the term used for the final lettering and decorating of the book; until this point the book has been 'forwarded'. Finishing presses are smaller than lying presses, but they should still be sturdy and well made as it is very important that the book should be held firmly while it is being tooled. Finishing presses are placed on the bench while in use and do not have a tub of their own. It is perfectly possible to use your lying press as a finishing press, but not vice versa.

Board Cutter

It is possible to cut board with a strong knife, such as a Stanley knife, and a

Fig 12   Board cutter in a corner of the author's bindery.

22

Fig 13   The board cutter in use.

Fig 14   A small card cutter.

straight edge, or a plough, but the convenience of a board cutter is immeasurable. The ideal board cutter is made of cast iron, the blade is hinged and the board or paper to be cut is laid on the iron bed and held in place by the foot-operated clamp. There is also a moveable guide which runs along the groove in the centre of the bed, with a long edge parallel to the blade. It can be screwed into position thus ensuring not only an accurate cut but also that one measurement can be repeated.

Unfortunately, board cutters are not only large, but extremely heavy and are perhaps not entirely suited to a small home bindery. However, there are alternatives: table board or card cutters, consisting of a blade and bed with a hand-operated clamp and gauge. These will,

23

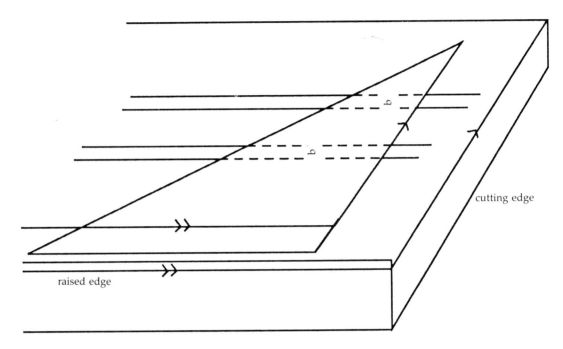

Fig 15 Bench board cutter.

however, cut only thin board, and as the clamp is hand-operated it is not as easy to hold the board in position while cutting (a friend could help here). The blades are usually not as heavy or strong as on a full-sized board cutter, and this could lead to inaccuracy due to the blade bending.

Perhaps the best alternative is to buy a weighted blade and cutting edge which can be attached to the end of your bench (different lengths of blades are available but the longer and stronger you can afford or accommodate the better). The bench end must be an accurate 90°, and a length of wood or metal screwed to the front edge of your bench at right-angles to the blade (accuracy is vital – much of a book-binder's time is spent trying to find or cut a right angle and 88° will *not* do) will provide a useful guideline. A wooden gauge running along a groove and se-cured by a wing nut (or for even greater accuracy two parallel grooves) would be an easily-made moveable guide, and a simple foot-operated clamp could also be devised.

Sewing Frame

I have included the sewing frame, or (as I have heard it described) 'harp', because although it is not absolutely necessary for sewing on tapes, which is how most cloth-covered books are sewn, you may come across an early cloth book which has been sewn on sunken cords for which a sewing frame is essential.

I think sewing frames are rather beauti-ful. They are also relatively simple – the book sits on the wooden bed while the tapes or cords are secured around the loose moveable wooden bar, and held in place through a ½in (1cm) slot in the bed immediately below the bar, by means of

Fig 16   Sewing frame.

Fig 17   Brass sewing keys – tape key on the left, cord key on the right.

brass sewing keys. The bar is raised or lowered by means of the two wooden 'nuts' on which it rests which screw up and down the two wooden posts.

Sewing frames come in different sizes, but if you have the choice it would be sensible to choose the largest available. It is also possible to make your own, and I have seen very successful ones made by students using metal rods and nuts instead of wooden ones. The important thing to remember is that the cords must be very taut when sewn on, so a lot of strain is put on the supporting bar. It must be mobile, as it is impossible to obtain the correct tension on the cords if it is immoveable.

Fig 18   A home-made sewing frame with tape and keys.

Nipping Press

Although it is possible to use your lying press as a nipping press, this is not very satisfactory as it can mean that your valuable lying press is out of action for some length of time. Soon you will be looking longingly at pictures of nipping presses and casting covetous glances at those belonging to your friends, college or tutor.

Standard nipping presses have platens measuring about 12 × 18in (30 × 45cm) with daylight – that is the maximum possible distance between the top and bottom platens – of 18–20in (45–50cm). As they are heavy they should stand on a sturdy bench, preferably over a supporting leg, and be screwed down, as they have a tendency to move as they are used.

It is not a good idea to buy a new nipping press as they are very expensive, and second-hand ones are usually available from bookbinding suppliers. It can also be fun, if you are in no particular hurry, to find your own. They can be discovered in scrap merchants' yards and junk shops, and I once came across *three* in the closing-down auction of a market garden business.

Should a nipping press not be available, an acceptable alternative is a document press. This is smaller and lighter than a nipping press and, although it is possible to find ones with large platens, usually not much larger than 15 × 10in (37.5 – 25cm). The main disadvantage is that the daylight is very meagre – usually about 3in (7.5cm) – which severely limits the

Fig 19   Nipping press.

size of book you can press. However, it is possible to overcome this by having the upright arms of the press lengthened by a good blacksmith or metalworker. In this case the top platen will obviously no longer close on to the lower bed, and it will be necessary to pad out the gap with extra boards for pressing small books and paper. Do make sure your press, particularly the platens, is free from rust and that the platens are smooth and clean before use.

Wooden 'hobby presses' are available, but lack the strength and stability of the iron ones which are altogether preferable.

Fig 20   Document press.

Finishing Stove

Whether you choose a gas or electric finishing stove is entirely a matter of personal preference, or, of course, the availability of either source of power. Gas stoves are favoured by many binders as the heat is more immediate and easy to control, and they can also be run from gas cylinders if you have no gas supply. An electric stove can take longer to heat up and if you are using one tool constantly this can be a disadvantage.

The stove consists of an outer indented

28

Fig 21   Finishing stove.

ring, on which the wooden tool handles rest, which circles the central heating plate on which the brass tool faces are heated. The temperature is controlled by a thermostat. It is possible to improvise a finishing stove, but great care must be taken to ensure that it is safe for both the binder and his tools.

Finishing Tools

Handle letters come in 40-piece sets – 26 letters, numbers 0 to 8 (6 usually doubles for 9), a comma, a full stop, two dipthongs and an ampersand, all neatly housed in a wooden box. There is a bewildering number of different typefaces and sizes. Type is measured in points, a point being 1/72 of an inch, and most bookbinders possess an assortment of sizes of the same typeface (this is important, because although it is permissible to use different sizes of letters on a book, it would not do to mix different styles), from 6 point to 36 point. As handle letters are expensive, your first (and possibly only set for some time) must be of the greatest possible use to you. Avoid, therefore, the very small and the very large, and choose either a 10 point or a 12 point alphabet. Similarly, your choice of typeface should be governed by how generally useful it will be – a good option would be a basic 'Roman' typeface such as York or Edinburgh, although a slightly thinner (more condensed) style such as Times Roman Condensed could also be

Fig 22   A 30 point alphabet.

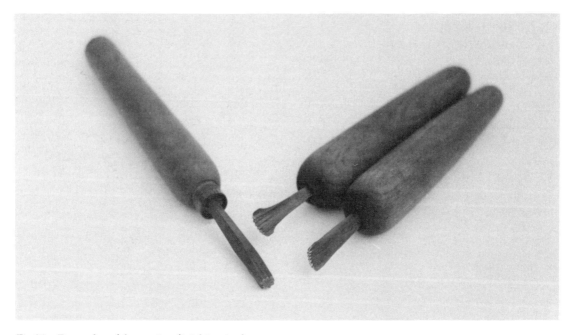

Fig 23   Examples of decorative finishing tools.

considered. The advantage of a condensed typeface is that it can fit more easily across the spine of the book, a point for serious consideration if you do not intend to invest in several different sizes. If you have a fairly traditional typeface, its use is far wider than that of a more modern one, which, however attractive it might be, would be wrong on anything but an equally modern book.

Finishing tools are made of brass which will retain heat and has a high melting point, but is a soft metal which will not harm leather. Beware of trying to heat lead type or adapt it for use as hand tools. Brass does, however, mark easily and great care must be taken of your tools – avoid dropping or scratching them as any imperfection on the face of the tool will be reflected in the tooling.

Decorative Tools

An infinite number of decorative tools is available, and a tool cutter will cut almost any tool to your own design. To begin with, particularly when working with foil on cloth, your needs will be modest. Very intricate tools are difficult to put down successfully on cloth, and you will find that you will have just as much, if not more, pleasure from making up patterns and designs with a few simple tools. It is perfectly possible to cut your own basic tools from lengths of brass rod set in wooden dowelling handles, using fine metal files.

Although you will not need many decorative tools to begin with, it is as well to be acquainted with those available. As with letters all line thicknesses are

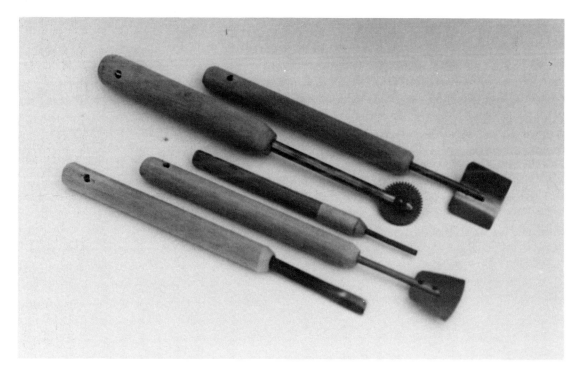

Fig 24   Home-made finishing tools.

measured in points, and it is advisable to have all your gouges, fillets and pallets the same point size.

Curved lines are called gouges. Each gouge is a fraction of a circle, and a set of gouges consists of portions or arcs of circles of different diameter, ranging from small tight curves to wider, almost flat ones. It is not necessary to buy gouges measuring more than ½in (1cm) in length – a short gouge can still make a long curve but a long gouge cannot make a short curve. Straight line tools are called pallets and also come in various lengths, starting from about ⅛in. Long spine pallets measuring 3in (7.5cm) and with a curved surface are for tooling across the rounded spines of books, and they are available not only as single or double lines, but also with decorations. In the beginning you

Fig 25   A simple design and the tools that were used in its creation.

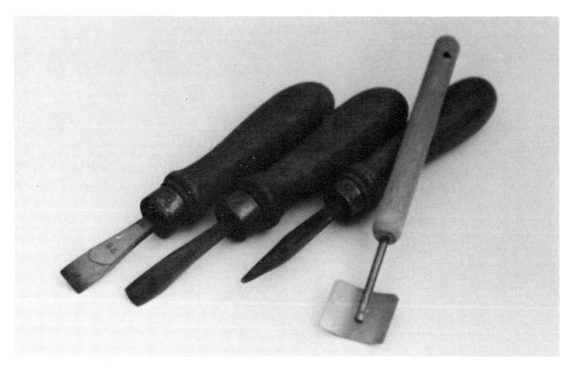

Fig 26   Gouges. The gouge on the extreme right was made at home by a student.

Fig 27   Pallets, from left to right, $\frac{5}{8}$in pallet, $\frac{1}{8}$in pallet, spine pallet and home-made pallet.

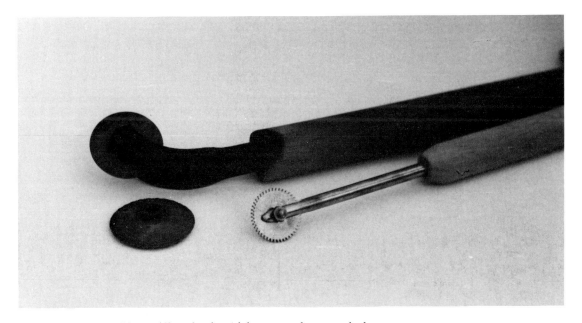

Fig 28   Fillets. Small brass fillet wheels with home-made one at the bottom.

will need only a single line. To tool long straight lines a brass wheel or fillet is used, and, as with the spine pallet, fillets are available with many different faces. A full-sized wheel is usually 3in (7.5cm) in diameter, but some tool cutters will make a smaller wheel which can not only be easier to handle but costs less.

Second-hand tools are available, but do make sure that the surfaces are not worn or damaged. Burnt handles can be re-placed, but check that the shafts that fit into the wooden handles are long enough to do their job properly – nothing is more annoying than a wobbly tool head that drops on to your book just as it is about to be put down. Old alphabets should be treated with equal caution. Remember that if you are to have more than one alphabet it is a good idea for the typeface to be the same, and also that it is often difficult to match old alphabets. Also check that all the letters are there and that they are not damaged in any way. I have noticed that the difference in price be-tween the old and the new finishing tools is not usually enough to make the risk worth while.

3 Materials

It is neither necessary nor practical for the amateur bookbinder to keep vast stores of materials. Many bookbinding suppliers will sell fairly small quantities of cloth and board, although if the order is to be posted there is sometimes a minimum value set. As with equipment, buy the best and most suited to your purpose that you can afford.

Looking through a supplier's catalogue you will see that the pH value of most materials is given particularly for paper and board. Materials tend to be either slightly acid or alkaline, and the degree is measured in a pH test on a scale of 0 to 14 – 0 to 6 shows varying degrees of acidity, and 8 to 14 degrees of alkalinity. Neutral is represented by 7 and therefore materials should ideally have a pH of as close to 7 as possible. Excess acidity or alkalinity will result in discoloration of paper and inks, and in severe cases will cause the paper to become brittle. As the main point of any binding, whether it is of leather or of cloth, is to protect the text, it is the binders' duty to ensure that he is not hastening the book's demise by using unsatisfactory material.

BOARD

Until the late sixteenth century the pages of books were protected by wooden boards, and the word 'board' is still used to describe the hard outer protective material. The first non-wooden boards were made by pasting sheets of paper together to form a thickness. Two main types of board are available to the binder today.

Grey-Board

This is a fairly soft board made from selected repulped paper pulp. It is ideal for cloth work.

Mill-Board

This is a harder, more dense board than grey-board with a smooth surface. Mill-board should be used when you are doing leather binding and good quality heavy cloth work.

Both the above boards are available in a variety of thicknesses from 1mm to 4mm. A supply of $\frac{1}{16}$th (1.5mm) and $\frac{1}{8}$th (3mm) board is the most useful combination, but if only one can be bought the most sensible purchase would be the thinner, as it can always be doubled or even trebled to make up the required thickness. Although not guaranteed acid-free, the pH of the paper pulp is monitored, while acid-free conservation board is available from some suppliers. Boards can be bought singly from good paper suppliers, although they are more usually bought in bundles by weight from board manufacturers (normally twenty 1.5mm boards per bundle, ten 3mm boards per bundle).

PAPER

Paper is a wonderful material which you will come to appreciate more as you work with it and become acquainted with some of the many different varieties. From the fourteenth century books were written or printed on hand-made paper, and one of the reasons that so many of them have survived is the excellent quality of this paper. When the Industrial Revolution and a greater spread of literacy and general education brought an increased demand for books, quicker and cheaper methods of book production were needed, so machines were devised to do the work originally done by hand. The first paper-making machines were developed first in France and then in England by the beginning of the nineteenth century.

Hand-Made Paper

The best quality and strongest papers are hand-made. A whole book could be written about paper making but a brief knowledge is useful, and should help towards an understanding of its various uses.

Paper is a 'substance composed of fibres interlaced into a compact web' (*Hand-made Paper Today*, Silvie Turner and Birgit Skiöld (Lund Humphries)). Although paper can technically be made from any cellulose material, from onion skins to nettle leaves, good hand-made paper is produced from a pulp made from cotton or linen. The actual sheet of paper is formed by the 'vat man', who dips a mould (over which is stretched a wire sieve or screen) into the vat of pulp. Excess water is drained away through the sieve, as the vat man gently shakes the mould in all directions, until he is left with a thin layer

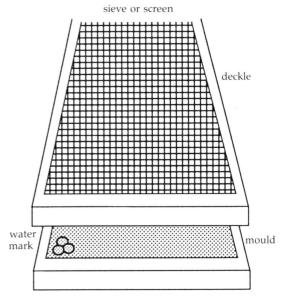

Fig 29   Mould and sieve for hand-made paper.

of intertwined fibres on the surface of the screen. The pulp is held in place by a moveable frame or 'deckle', and occasionally a second, finer screen is also placed on top of the pulp to facilitate drainage and ensure a more even distribution of the pulp.

You will often see paper described as 'laid' or 'wove', and this refers to the pattern left on the surface of the paper by the screen. Simply, laid screens have a mesh consisting of closely-spaced parallel wires, supported by wider-spaced parallel wires running at right angles. Wove screens were originally made from a woven cloth, and nowadays are made from thin 'woven' wire, producing a smoother paper with no laid lines. Watermarks showing the maker's symbol, sometimes the year, and either a hand or lettering to signify that the paper is hand-made, are also incorporated in the screen to be transferred to the paper at this stage.

Paper is strengthened and made less

absorbent by sizing. If the size (usually made from animal gelatine) is added to the pulp before the paper is formed, this is described as internal sizing; if the sheet of paper is sized after it has been formed and pressed it is described as being tub or surface sized. The words 'HP', 'not' and 'rough' beside a named sheet of paper in a catalogue indicate the type of surface. 'HP' stands for hot pressed – this paper has been passed through a series of hot or cold polished rollers to give it a hard, shiny surface; paper which has not been hot pressed is described logically enough as 'not' – the surface of this paper has been smoothed by pressing, but is not as hard or shiny as the surface produced by the HP process; finally 'rough' indicates a textured surface.

As hand-made sheets are made in individual moulds, the edges of the paper are not cut or trimmed as they are taken from the mould to be pressed and dried. This untrimmed edge is known as a 'deckle edge', presumably because it is formed by pulp which has seeped under the enclosing frame known as the 'deckle'.

Hand-made paper gains its strength and durability from the quality of the basic materials, the length of the fibre and the fact that the fibres are shaken in all directions.

Machine-Made Paper

Nowadays the only books produced on hand-made paper are limited edition private press books, or specially-commissioned books. Commercially-produced books are usually printed on machine-made or, occasionally, mould-made paper.

The first paper-making machine was invented in France by Nicholas-Louis Robert in the late eighteenth century, and the machine was refined and developed in England by John Gamble and Henry and Seule Fourdrinier. The first paper mill using the Fourdrinier machine was opened in 1801 and by 1830 more paper was made by machine than by hand in Great Britain and abroad.

In the Fourdrinier machine pulp from the vat flows on to an endless wire gauze web, through which the excess water drains, aided by a vacuum pump. Although the web ensures the even distribution of the pump, its speed and inability to shake the fibres in all directions as with hand-made paper causes the fibres to run mainly in one direction, which means that machine-made paper has a grain. The importance of this grain direction will be discussed later. Felt rollers pass over the pulp to dry and consolidate it further, after which the endless roll of paper is passed over rollers where it is dried and finished and finally rolls on to a reel as finished paper.

Machine-made paper differs from hand-made paper in many ways. Machine-made paper does not always have a watermark or laid lines, although these can be impressed on the paper by means of a dandy roll under which the paper is passed, and the edges are not deckled. Although some machine-made paper is made from good quality pulp, poor quality cheaper paper is also produced, mainly using wood pulp which tends to be acid.

Mould-Made Paper

You will find that, although a small stock of hand-made paper is useful, much of your work involves the use of mould-made paper. This is made by revolving a partially-immersed cylinder in a vat of pulp, thus creating a vacuum inside the cylinder and causing the pulp to adhere to the outside which is covered with a metal screen or mould cover. This can be either wove or laid and carry a watermark, thus giving many mould-made papers the appearance of being hand-made. As with machine-made papers the fibres run mainly in one direction so that mould-made papers also have a grain. A deckle is formed on the two outer edges of the paper, while the other two have a cut edge. From the cylinder the paper is passed through rollers; and in this way it is dried and pressed.

Size

It is useful to understand both the imperial measurements of paper as well as the new metric ones.

Traditional Sizes

- Foolscap   17 × 13½in
- Crown   15 × 20in
- Demy   17½ × 22½in
- Imperial   20 × 30in
- Double Elephant   27 × 40in

These sizes can also be made twice the size, in which case the shorter side is doubled:

- Double Crown   30 × 20in
- Double Demy   .   35 × 22½in
- Double Imperial   40 × 30in

Or quadruple sizes, in which again the shorter side of the double size is doubled:

- Quadruple Crown   30 × 40in
- Quadruple Demy   35 × 45in

Metric Sizes

The International Standards Organisation (ISO) decided that it would be easier if all paper sizes were standardised. The sizes for printing and writing papers are known as A sizes and are based on the sub-division of one square metre of paper to form the following paper sizes.

- A0   1189 × 841mm
- A1   841 × 594mm
- A2   594 × 420mm
- A3   420 × 297mm
- A4   297 × 210mm
- A5   210 × 148mm

Unfortunately these paper sizes did not adapt themselves very comfortably to book production, so standard metric sizes which were considered suitable for book production were introduced.

- Metric Crown Octavo   186 × 123mm
- Metric Large Crown Octavo   189 × 129mm
- Metric Demy Octavo   216 × 138mm
- Metric Royal Octavo   234 × 156mm

Weight

The thickness of a sheet of paper is judged by its weight, which is calculated by the number of grams per square metre. Therefore a paper weighing 100 grams per square metre (100gsm) is lighter and thinner than one weighing 150gsm.

Translating Information

If you were to read the following description of a paper in a catalogue:

'Hand-made/Flax Cotton, internally sized/wove/not surface, 150gsm'

you will be dealing with a hand-made paper from a flax and cotton pulp to which the size was added, with a wove surface which has not been hot pressed and therefore is not particularly shiny, weighing 150 grams per square metre.

Buying and Storing

When repairing or rebinding a book it is often necessary to introduce new paper. This should be as sympathetic to the original as possible, matching it in colour, weight and surface as closely as you can. Note whether the original has any laid lines or whether it has a wove surface, if it has a shiny, hot-pressed finish or not, and whether it is mould-made or hand-made, and choose your paper accordingly. By buying a few extra sheets at a time it is possible to build up a fairly comprehensive supply. Good hand-made and mould-made paper and most repair papers are available from specialist paper suppliers, most of whom are willing to send orders through the post, although most do have a minimum order requirement. To begin with, however, your local art shop should be able to furnish you with your basic needs. The following list is a suggested beginning for your paper stock.

Ingres

This useful paper is available from most good art shops. Although it is made in several different weights most shops stock only 90gsm and 160gsm. A wide range of colours is available, including whites and creams and a very useful shade of 'dirty cream' which blends well with older books, and there are also laid and wove surfaces. You will usually find that most shops stock either a Fabriano or a Canson Ingres.

Cartridge

A small supply of good quality machine-made cartridge paper, preferably slightly off-white, is useful.

Repair Papers

Of the many repair papers available the following will provide a good basis for the start of your stock:

Kozushi A cream Japanese tissue, available as hand-made or machine-made, the former being more expensive but stronger than the latter.

Tengujo A thinner Japanese tissue, used for repairing, strengthening and backing paper. Both kozushi and tengujo papers, although thin, are very strong, particularly when they are hand-made as they are mainly produced from long-fibred plants.

Crompton tissue A thin tissue backed with a heat-sensitive adhesive which is used for repair work where a dry repair is necessary. Crompton tissue is very convenient, but unfortunately it seems to be available only in large rolls, a lifetime's supply for most home binders. It is available from specialist paper and archivist suppliers only.

Kraft Paper

From the German word for 'strength', Kraft paper is used for lining spines and is strong brown paper.

Manila

Manila looks like thin card and is available in different weights, the most useful being 225gsm.

Decorative Papers

For most cloth work plain-coloured Ingres paper is not only adequate but more appropriate than a highly decorative paper as an endpaper.

Marbled paper The best quality marbled paper is hand-marbled on to a good machine- or mould-made paper. The marbler floats the colours on to a size and literally draws his pattern on the surface, allowing the design to develop not only from his own manipulation of the colours but also from the spread and positioning of the various inks. Nowadays many beautiful modern designs are produced, although the most useful to the bookbinder are the reproductions of older designs. These are more appropriate for repairing or rebinding older books where it is most important to use the correct type of marbling, as various styles were developed and produced at different dates. A cheaper alternative to hand-marbled paper is machine-marbled or printed paper.

Printed papers Papers covered with a repeated all-over pattern can make an attractive covering material for a half or quarter binding.

Decorative hand-mades Some of the most original and beautiful papers have evolved from simply using the fibres from which the papers are made as a decorative device. Many of them are Japanese, and, although their delicacy does not make them particularly suitable for cloth work,

you should be aware of their existence. Sturdier hand-mades also include natural fibres, dried flowers and leaves as well as coloured, gold or silver flecks.

Making your own decorative paper is great fun and can be very rewarding, particularly if it is done for a special binding.

The papers mentioned by name here represent a tiny fraction of those available. You will also become acquainted with Bodleian and Dover paper, with Abbey Mills and Glastonbury and many more, as the need arises. Most suppliers will send you their catalogue and price list along with any relevant samples you may require and you will usually find them very helpful.

CLOTH

Although in theory it is possible to cover a book in virtually any material, in practice those specially prepared for the job are the best.

Book Cloth

This is a strongly-woven cloth usually from cotton or linen. To prevent the glue from filtering through the weave of the cloth it is specially treated with a starch filler, but even so you should beware of pressing freshly-glued cloth. Others have a tissue or paper lining. A wide range of colours is available and it is possible to buy fairly small quantities. The minimum length from most suppliers is one metre. For most of the cloth work described here a book cloth such as 'Reliance' will be suitable.

Buckram

This is generally recognised as the strongest and best quality cloth, to be used particularly for large cloth bindings where strength is needed.

Rexine

This is a strong cotton cloth with a nitro-cellulose coating which renders it, if not completely waterproof, at least water-repellent and more resistant to staining than book cloth. It too is available in a wide range of colours, weights (210gsm and 250gsm), and a variety of embossed grains.

Paper Cloth

You will come across this hybrid in suppliers' lists, probably as 'Linson'. It is really a strong paper with an embossed cloth grain. It is less strong and durable than cloth.

MULL

A supply of mull is essential. It is used for lining the spines of books and is a coarsely-woven muslin, whose open weave allows the glue to penetrate.

SEWING MATERIALS

The first cloth-cased bindings were sewn on sunken cords, nowadays it is more usual to sew on tapes. You will come across books with neither cords nor tapes, but this practice is not encouraged.

Cord

Although sewing on cords is usually associated with leather bindings, some early cloth books were sewn on thin sunken cords. Cord is made either from hemp or linen, and the best quality cord is made from the latter with its long fibres contributing to the strength and smoothness of the cord. The yarn is twisted into thin strands or 'plies' of cord, and the plies are then further twisted together in varying multiples to form different thicknesses of cord from 4 ply to 27 ply. The most useful ply to buy is 8 or 12 ply – it is doubtful if you will need thicker cord than 12 ply for a leather binding and it can always be reduced to the required thinness for smaller leather books or cased bindings.

Tape

Made from cotton or linen, tape comes in rolls of different widths, the most useful being $\frac{1}{2}$in (1cm), although a thinner and a thicker one would be a helpful addition to your supplies.

Thread

Best quality linen thread should be used. This is available in skeins of varying thicknesses, from thin two-strand to medium three-strand and thick four-strand. The medium three-strand is the most useful, although as you do more binding the addition of a thinner and a thicker thread will become necessary.

ADHESIVES

Any adhesive you use must not only have a neutral pH – there is little point in ensuring that your materials are acid-free if you are going to stick them together with an acidic glue or paste – but should also be reversible. Preferably, use adhesives that are soluble in water, rather than relying on chemical solvents – this is not just to make the rectifiying of your mistakes easier, but is an aid to future binders who may have to do further work on the binding.

Hot Glue

This is animal glue, available either in a slab or as pearl glue, which is dissolved in water and heated in a double glue pot. Until fairly recently hot glue was widely used, but with the advent of cold flexible glues (polyvinyl acetates), it now tends to be used in small binderies for special work only. Although it is easily reversible hot glue is less convenient to use than the prepared cold glues and is less flexible when dry.

Cold Glue

Polyvinyl acetate or PVA is the most commonly used commercially-prepared glue. There are many forms of this glue and it is important to buy one specially prepared for bookbinding from a reliable supplier of adhesives. You can buy PVA in large 5-litre tubs, but, unless you are going to share it between several friends, a smaller half-litre tub will do to start with. PVA will keep well at room temperature, but it does not like to be below freezing point, and if it is left with the lid off it will form a thick skin – although this is easy enough to remove it is a waste of glue. PVA tends to thicken after some time but this can be easily remedied by the careful addition of a little water to the required consistency.

The main advantages of PVA are that it is already prepared, it is soluble in water, and it remains flexible when dry.

Paste

As a general rule, glue is used for sticking cloth, covering materials (apart from leather), and glueing the spines of books, and paste, which is a wetter adhesive, is used for paper (unless it is a covering paper). Commercially-produced starch-based paste with preservatives can be bought from suppliers, but it is quite easy to make your own (*see* page 148).

FOIL

Coloured foils for lettering can be bought from most bookbinding suppliers or direct from manufacturers. Silver and gold coloured foils are available in lengths of about 100ft (30m) on spools, in widths varying from 1in (2.5cm) upwards – 4in (10cm) is a useful width. The foil has a heat-sensitive adhesive on the back which, when the foil is tooled with a warm finishing tool will result in the tool's impression being left on the surface. Although real gold foil is available, foils are really only suitable for cloth work – they can be used on leather, but tend to look brassy when compared with gold leaf.

WASTE PAPER

I think the most jealously-guarded thing in my workshop is my pile of printer's waste – this is paper discarded by a printer, and used for covering my bench tops to ensure a clean working surface, and for pressing and drying. This is invaluable as the print will not come off and transfer itself – old magazines and newspapers should be avoided because of this tendency. If your local printer is not obliging, old posters (provided they are not creased) can be used. Computer paper can be useful too, although it usually has to be used doubled or trebled, both to guard against the print and because it is rather thin. Remember that any marks or creases on your waste paper, particularly if it is being used for drying or pressing, will always transfer to your book or paper.

4 The Parts of a Book and History

The primary function of binding a book is to protect the printed pages – if it is also decorative and pleasing to the eye, this is of course a bonus. In describing the various parts of a book, I will start from the outside and work inwards. Although I am dealing here with cloth-covered books, the same terms also apply to leather-bound books.

The hard outer covers of the book are called the 'boards'. In early bindings they were made of wood, but they are now usually grey-board, mill-board or (occasionally) straw-board. The boards protect the vulnerable inner parts of the book and should be slightly larger than the book itself. The amount that the boards project from the leaves is called the 'square', and usually the square is equal to the thickness of the board – so a very small book may have a square of only $\frac{1}{16}$in (1.5mm), while a large heavy book with thick boards will have a correspondingly larger square. The average square is $\frac{1}{8}$in (2.5mm).

You will hear cloth-covered books referred to as 'cased bindings'. This is because the case or outer cover of the book, which is composed of two boards and a spine stiffener covered with cloth, is made separately from the book, and the two are put together as a final action. In a leather-bound book the boards are actually attached to the book before covering, thus making a much stronger binding.

A book covered entirely in cloth is described as 'full cloth'.

In a 'half cloth' book, only the spine and corners are covered in cloth, and the remaining areas of the boards are covered with paper. An alternative to covering the spine and corners is to cover the spine and have a strip of cloth along the front edge or 'foredge' of the book – this is called a 'foredge strip'.

If the book is 'quarter cloth', only the spine is covered in cloth, and the rest of the boards are covered in paper. This is a cheaper form of covering and not very satisfactory as the corners of the book, covered in a weaker material, remain vulnerable. This problem can be remedied by putting on very small cloth corners, or 'tips', but if you are going to this trouble you might just as well do a half cloth binding.

The back of the book is called the 'spine' and the front edge the 'foredge'. The top of the book is the 'head' and the bottom is the 'tail'. Sometimes you will find a coloured strip at the head and tail of cloth books, and these are the 'head bands'. Head bands are always present in a leather-bound book, where they consist of a core made from leather, glued string or (occasionally) rolled paper, around which coloured silks are wound. They are actually sewn into the book, and in a leather-bound book they perform both a structural and decorative function. In

Fig 30   Full and half cloth books.

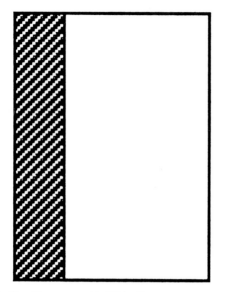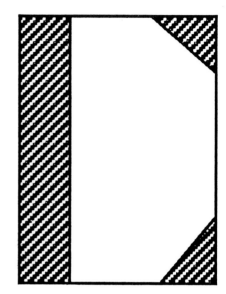

Fig 31   Quarter and half bindings.

cloth bindings they are purely decorative; for this purpose you can buy an infinite variety of different-coloured headbands by the metre which are simply cut to size and glued to the spine of the book. They make a pleasing addition to the general appearance and finish of a cased binding.

The other important thing to be found on the outside is the title of the book and name of its author. Both should be read easily. Although the traditional way to letter a book is across the spine, the spine is often too narrow to accommodate the words without either splitting them up several times or using an uncomfortably small typeface. In this case, it is acceptable and indeed preferable to letter either up or down the spine. As with every other decision to be made in bookbinding, the size and age of the book must be taken into consideration when choosing the type and size of letter and the way in which the book is to be titled.

As the front (or upper) board is opened the 'endpapers' are revealed. As their name implies, these are the papers at each end of the book. The paper that is stuck to the board is the 'paste-down' or 'board paper', and facing it is the 'free endpaper' or 'first fly leaf'. Any subsequent blank sheets are known as the 'second fly leaf', and so on. There are many different types of endpaper, as you will discover, and, as with everything else, it is important to use the correct style for the age, type and size of book. The endpapers introduce the reader to the book and so the 'white' papers, as opposed to the coloured or decorative papers (the term 'white' can cover any shade from brilliant white to dirty cream) should be compatible with the pages of the book, being as similar in weight, colour and texture as possible.

Now to the printed book itself. If you look at the head of your book at the spine edge you will see that the pages of the book form gatherings or 'sections'. In some modern books and paperbacks the backs of the sections are chopped off to leave the book composed of separate sheets of paper held together by glue. These 'perfect' bindings will be dealt with later. A section was once a whole sheet of paper on which the various pages of the book were printed before it was folded. Correctly placing the blocks of type upon the sheet so that when it is printed and folded they will fall into sequence is called 'imposition'.

You may have heard of a book being described as a folio, quarto or octavo. These terms refer to the type of section and the number of leaves forming the section from the original sheet of paper. A section made from folding the paper once in half is called a 'folio'; if it is folded again it becomes a quarto (4to), with four leaves and eight printed sides; another fold and it is an octavo (8vo), and so on to 16mo and occasionally 32mo. Thus a book described as a Crown Octavo has sections consisting of eight leaves with sixteen printed sides, made from a Crown size piece of paper. Most books nowadays are trimmed and ready to read but it is still possible to find old uncut or partially-cut

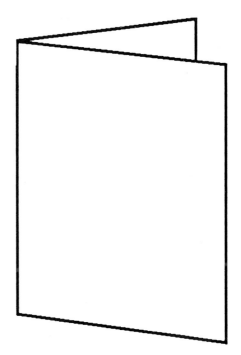

Fig 33   Folio.

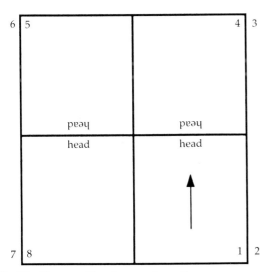

Fig 32   Page position for quarto section.

Fig 34   Quarto.

books (the latter being presumably one where the reader lost interest!).

To help the binder, the sections of a book usually have a small letter or signature placed discreetly at the bottom of the first page of each section. These run alphabetically, so the first section will be marked A, the second B, and so on. Sometimes I or J are omitted as they could be confused, either with the number 1 or with each other. When there are more than twenty-six sections the alphabet is begun again but this time the letters are doubled – Aa, Bb – or even trebled (Aaa). The signatures are a great help when the book is being sewn together – it is far easier to check that B follows A than to read what is written on one page and make sure that the following writing makes sense, particularly if you are not well acquainted with the subject. It is also a great help when you are pulling the book apart; again, it is easier to look for the signatures than to count pages.

A further help to the binder, only apparent when the book is in pieces, are small black marks sometimes put along the bolts or back folds of the sections. When the book is sewn in the correct order these marks form a graduated pattern up the spine of the book, so that any section sewn upside-down or in the wrong place can easily be spotted.

A BRIEF HISTORY

There are many excellent books on the subject of the history of bookbinding, but you should know a little about the background to cloth-covered books.

Until the end of the eighteenth century a book was sewn on five cords, with the boards being laced on to the ends (or slips) of these cords. The boards were thus part of the book itself, and the book was then covered in leather. By the end of the eighteenth century, however, education had become more widespread and, with an ever-widening reading public, the demand for books increased.

Printers tried to keep pace with the increased demand and the advent of the first steam press in 1812 by Koenig and Bauer, and the invention in France of a paper-making machine by Louis Robert (commercialised in England five years later) led to many more books being produced. This in turn resulted in the

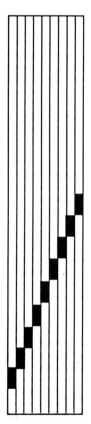

Fig 35 Graduated marks along the backs of sections.

need for quicker and cheaper ways of binding books.

The first cloth bindings appeared in about 1825. These books were still sewn on cords although the cords were 'sawn in'. This means that channels were sawn into the spine of the book, rather like the cerfs sawn for the kettle stitches, and the thin cords slotted neatly into these channels. Later tapes were used – altogether a stronger and more satisfactory method.

The idea of casing books was then developed. The case or protective cover, consisting of two boards and a spine piece covered with cloth, was made separately from the book and the book was 'cased in' as a final operation.

5 Single-Section Binding

As the name implies, a single section is a book made from one piece of paper folded to form a single section. The following method of binding is also used to protect printed single-section pamphlets and catalogues.

PREPARATIONS

Make sure that your bench or table is clean and uncluttered; ideally you should have enough room to spread out the sheet of paper from which you are going to make your single section. Cover your working surface with clean waste paper – it is a good idea to have two or three sheets, provided that the surface remains flat, so that if the top sheet becomes soiled it can be removed quickly and easily. Try to keep your hand tools within easy reach, and keep a pile of smaller sheets of waste paper near, with a cloth to wipe your fingers on as necessary. The idea is to be able to concentrate on what you are doing, without unnecessary searches for bone folders or dividers, or, even worse, having to leave a pasted sheet of paper curling itself up while you frantically look for some clean waste paper.

With everything ready and to hand, take your piece of clean new paper. It is very important to establish grain direction and to make sure that the grain of paper and board all run the same way – from head to tail. Imagine the fibres of machine-made paper and board to be flexible rods running from head to tail. Obviously fewer 'rods' or fibres will be broken by folding with the grain than against it, so a book will be stronger if the fibres or grain of its paper run from head to tail than from spine to foredge.

When paper is dampened the spaces between the fibres swell, causing the paper to expand widthways. When a sheet of hand-made paper is dampened it stretches in all directions, but machine-made papers and mould-made papers expand in one direction only – across the grain. If you were to paste a piece of paper to a piece of board with different grain directions, the ensuing expansions and contractions would result in a most peculiar and distorted board. This also explains the wavy edges of some books that have been left in a damp atmosphere – the dampness has not penetrated to the cen-

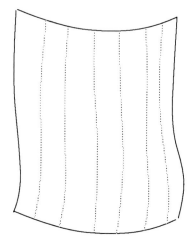

Fig 36　The direction of the grain.

tre of the book, resulting in uneven expansion of the paper and the cockling of the outer edges of the book.

There are several ways of finding out which way the grain runs on your paper:

• Hold the sheet up to the light and you should see the laid lines running parallel almost 1in (2.5cm) apart. Running at right angles to the laid lines there will sometimes be finer, closer lines. The grain of the paper usually runs in the same direction as the wider-spaced lines.

• Gently fold your paper over (do not crease it) longways and then shortways. You will find that there is more resistance when you fold across the grain than when the fold is with the grain. When the fold is with the grain you are folding with the main fibre direction, but across the grain the fibres are being bent and broken. This method of detecting grain direction is particularly useful for board. Cut a square-shaped piece of board and by bending the board first one way and then the other you can determine the direction of the grain.

• If the paper is fine, for example, a tissue, the grain may not be found easily by folding. If you dampen a corner of the paper it will expand across the grain, and as the sheet dries the expanded area will cockle and the edge at the corner curl around.

• If all else fails, tear a corner or sample piece of the paper first one way and then the other. The paper will tear more easily and in a straighter line with the grain than against it.

Paper and board are described as having either 'long grain' or 'short grain'. Long grain means that the grain of the paper runs along the longest side measurement, short grain that the grain is along the shortest side measurement.

You will find that when folding a 16mo section a long grain piece of paper is preferable to a short grain one. The eventual section will be either long- or short-grained, after the original sheet, if the grain is running correctly head to tail. Thus a long grain sheet of paper will produce a portrait-shaped, long-grained section and a short-grained piece of paper will produce a landscaped section. For a

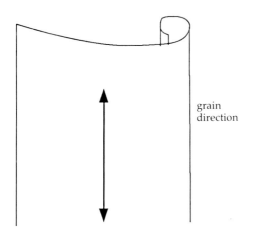

grain direction

Fig 37   Finding the correct grain direction.

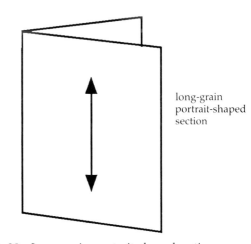

long-grain portrait-shaped section

Fig 38   Long-grain, portrait-shaped section.

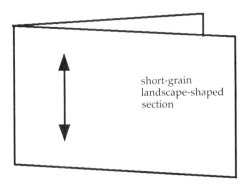

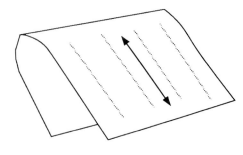

Fig 39   Short-grain, landscape-shaped section.

Fig 40

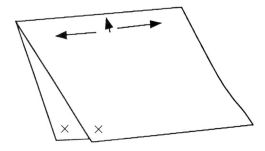

Fig 41

slim volume neither shape has any particular advantage, except that for a notebook the portrait shape is more convenient and traditional. For larger heavier books the landscaped shape is less suitable as more strain is put on the joints of the book.

SINGLE-SECTION BINDING

1. Find the grain of your paper, and mark it with a discreet pencil mark.
2. Lay the sheet of paper flat on the table in front of you. Fold it in half across the grain. Careful and accurate folding makes life much easier, so, to ensure as accurate a fold as possible:

(i)   Fold, or rather bend the paper over towards you *across* the grain (Fig 40).
(ii)   Line the two bottom right-hand corners up and ensure that the two edges marked × in Fig 41 are exactly together.
(iii)   Holding the folded sheet in position with your left hand, take up your bone folder and gently work along the fold, starting from the middle and working outwards (Fig 41).

Tools	Equipment	Materials
Pencil	Two pressing boards	Waste paper covering working surface
Dividers	Light weight ½lb/200g	Pile of waste paper for pasting
Scalpel – No. 10 blade	Nipping press	Pile of good quality waste for pressing
Straight edge		Board ⅛in thick
Bone folder		Book cloth
Glue and paste brushes		Decorative paper
Set square		Glue
Sharp knife		Paste
Needle and thread		Mull
		3-strand thread

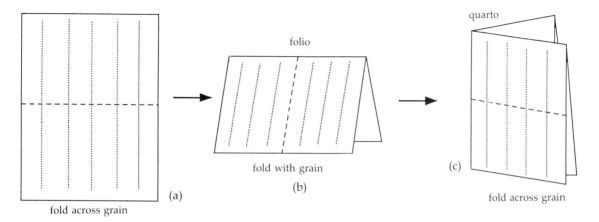

quarto

folio

fold with grain

(a)

(b)

(c)

fold across grain

fold across grain

Fig 42   Folding a sheet of paper. (a) Fold across the grain, then (b) with the grain, then (c) across the grain again.

(iv)   Place a sheet of clean waste over the fold and rub firmly with your bone folder through the waste to ensure a sharp fold. By working through the waste you will avoid marking your paper. You have now folded the paper in half and have a folio.

(v)   With the folded edge to your right, bend the folio over, this time folding *with* the grain. Make sure that the two already folded edges are absolutely together.

(vi)   Holding the paper in position with your left hand, work your bone folder gently but firmly along the new fold, this time starting from the right-hand corner to the left (to avoid trapping air in the folds and causing creases).

(vii)   Sharpen the fold by working with your bone folder through the waste sheet. You now have a quarto.

(viii)   Repeat the above, folding *across* the grain, so that you have an octavo.

(ix)   Repeat folding with the grain for a 16mo section.

You may find that after folding your paper into an octavo you have difficulty in folding it for the last time. To prevent damaging the paper, slit the edge you are about to fold (which will eventually be the head

of the book) with your bone folder. Do not try to cut all the paper at once or it will tear, but cut through one fold at a time. You will then find that your final fold is easier to accomplish.

3.   Put your book under a light weight while you cut the boards for it. When leaving books under a weight, select a pair of pressing boards larger than your book and cut two pieces of clean waste paper, again larger than the book, to line the pressing boards and to protect the book. Make a sandwich of the boards, waste paper and book with the weight placed so that it is central to the book. Before you place the book under the weight (particularly in this case where the pages are separate), make sure that the pages are all in place by holding the book lightly with both hands and tapping the spine gently on the bench, actually releasing your hold of the book as it touches the bench surface. Do the same with the head of the book. This will allow any section that has moved to drop back into place.

4.   Cut a pair of boards ½in (1cm) wider and ½in (1cm) longer than your book.

(i)   Find the grain of your board – remember that it must run from head to tail.

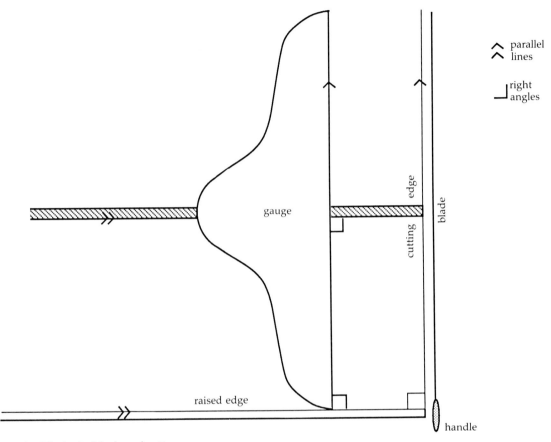

parallel
lines

right
angles

gauge

cutting edge

blade

raised edge

handle

Fig 43   The bed of the board cutter.

(ii)   Much of a bookbinder's time is spent
in the pursuit of right angles, which can
be very elusive; your boards *must* all have
corners of 90°. A board cutter is obviously
the best implement for cutting board,
although a knife and straight edge, or
later a plough, can be used. A board cutter
has a flat bed with a moveable gauge
which is parallel to the blade; both are at
right angles to the side of the cutter, facing
the binder.
(iii)   If you have a large sheet of board,
cut it to a manageable size.
(iv)   You now need one known straight
side to your board – the best way of being
certain of this is to cut it yourself.

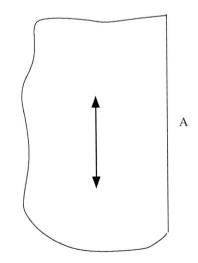

A

Fig 44

54

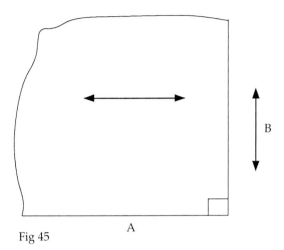

Fig 45

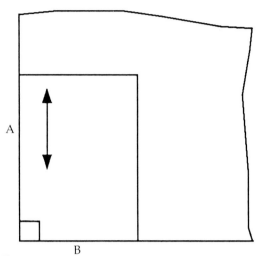

Fig 46

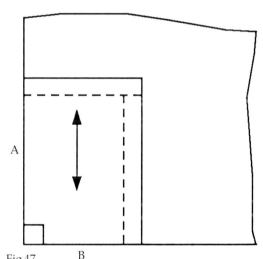

Fig 47

(v)   Having done this, move the gauge to the end of the bed away from the blade as you do not need it for the next cut. Place your known straight edge of board (A in Fig 44) against the raised edge of the board chopper so that the edge of the board (B) is beneath the blade. Cut. You now have a right angle which you should mark. You should now have a piece of board with two straight sides and one known right angle, and are ready to mark out and cut the boards for your book (Fig 45).

(vi)   Whenever possible avoid measuring your book with a ruler and then transferring the measurements to the board or paper – measurements always seem to change in mid-air. It is much better to work from the book itself.

(vii)   Place your single section on the board so that the cut edge and the spine of the book are on the known right angle of the board. Using a sharp pencil, mark the length and width of the book to the widest and longest page. Use a sharp pencil – when you are dealing with small, accurate measurements, a thick pencil line can make a great difference. If you have good eyesight and a light touch a scalpel blade can be used for marking lines on board.

(viii)   The boards need to be ½in (1cm) longer and ½in (1cm) wider than the book at this stage. Take your dividers and set them to ½in, add a ½in margin to the width and length of the outline on your board, and join the marks using a ruler and pencil (Figs 46 and 47).

(ix)   Place your board on the board chopper with side A against the gauge and B

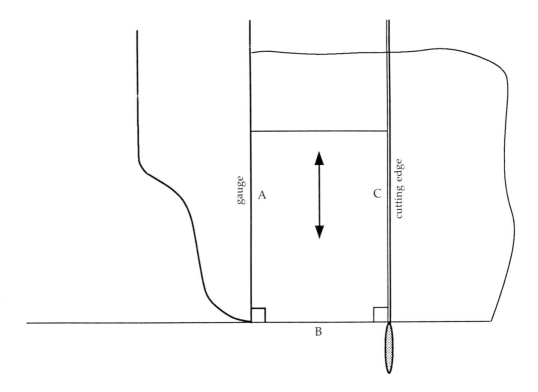

Fig 48

against the raised edge of the cutter. Move the gauge and board across the bed until the cutting line C is directly beneath the blade. Clamp and cut. You should now have a board of the required width with two known right angles (Figs 48 and 49).

(x) Now that the gauge is set to the desired width, cut your second board to the same width.

(xi) Move the gauge back and place the board on the bed, this time with side B against the gauge, and C against the raised edge, so that the remaining uncut edge (D) is beneath the blade. Move the gauge and the board until the cutting line D is directly beneath the blade. Clamp and cut. Repeat with the second board (Fig 50).

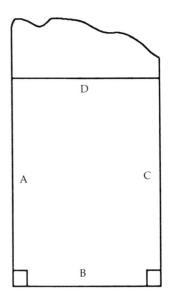

Fig 49

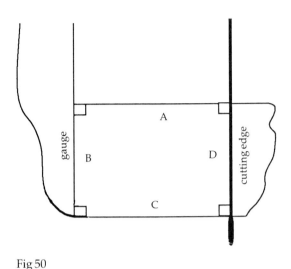

Fig 50

(xii)   You should now have two match-ing square boards ('square' meaning hav-ing corners of 90° even though the boards themselves are rectangular). Check that the boards are the same by turning them head to tail and knocking them level. At the long side and the head they should still fit together perfectly.

If you do not have access to a board cutter, and have to use a knife and straight edge, the same techniques for establishing a right angle can be used, although careful measurement and the use of a set square and/or L-square are necessary.
5.   Remove the single section from be-neath its weight and place between its boards. Gently knock it level at the head and spine. The importance of cutting your boards accurately will now be apparent, as the book will to some extent follow the shape of the boards. If the boards are cut badly, you are starting to build a lop-sided book. Mark on your boards which is the head of the book and with the head to your right:

(i)   Place the book carefully in your lying press, making sure that the book is in the centre of the press so that the pressure from the screws is even, with about 2in (5cm) of spine protruding. The screws should be just tight enough to hold the book securely. When putting a book in the press, hold the book in your left hand in the centre and gently tighten the screws, each one a little at a time.
(ii)   Using your dividers and pencil, mark the spine of the book up for sewing. However carefully you folded your paper there will inevitably be some variation in the length and width. After sewing you are going to trim the book to the length and width of the shortest page, and this trimming has to be taken into considera-tion when marking the spine up for sew-ing.
(iii)   Set your dividers to 1in, measure 1in from the head of the book and mark it with your pencil. Measure $1\frac{1}{4}$in up from the tail and mark. Divide the distance between the two marks and mark this mid point. You will now have three sewing marks on the spine of your book – a, c, and b (see Fig 51(a)). Divide the distances between a and c and c and b in half, and mark these two new points (d and e in Fig 51(b)). For single-section sewing an odd number of sewing holes is essential – five is adequate for most books, although a particularly long pamphlet may need seven or even nine.

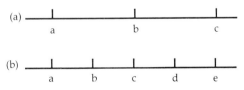

Fig 51   (a) and (b) Marking up a single section for sewing.

57

6. Take the book out of the press and carefully prick through the sewing marks with a needle, working from the inside. It is important that the needle goes straight through the centre of the folds – you will find this is made a little easier if you avoid the temptation to open the book fully while making the holes.

7. A strip of mull is used to strengthen the spine of your book. If you cut a paper template first, then place it on the mull and cut around it with scissors, you will find that this can avoid waste. The mull should overlap the spine of the book by 1in (2.5cm) on each side, so needs to be 2in (5cm) wide. The length of the mull is less than the entire length of the spine, and it should cover the head and tail stitches (a and b) by ½in (1cm). Mitre the corners of your mull strip and place it over the spine of your book, holding it in place with glue so that it cannot move while you are sewing. The sewing holes should still be visible through the mull, but if you are doubtful mark them with a pencil.

8. Thread your needle and, working from the inside to the outside, insert the needle in hole c. Pull the thread through, leaving a tail of about 2in (5cm) on the inside. Continue as follows:

Back into the book at d.
Out at a.
Back into the book through d.
Out through e.
Back into the book through c, arranging the thread so that it is on the opposite side of the long stitch from the 2in (5cm) tail which is already there.

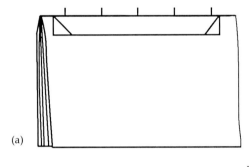

(a)

(b)

(c)

Fig 52   (a), (b) and (c) Lining the spine with mull.

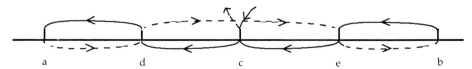

a   d   c   e   b

Fig 53   Sewing the single section.

Before tying the two threads together, check that your sewing is neither too loose nor too tight: with loose sewing the sections will move about, but on the other hand, if the sewing is too tight the spine of the book will be pulled from head to tail. When you are satisfied with the tension of your sewing, tie the two ends together with a reef knot. Trim the ends to ½in (1cm) and arrange them so that they are lying flat along the fold.

9.   Trim your book using a straight edge and scalpel (No. 10 blade). You will find an L-square or set square useful in helping you to cut the book accurately. Using the same principles as when cutting your board square, work from your one known straight edge, which will be the fold or spine edge of your book. Trim the head first.

Mark on the outside the amount necessary to dispose of all the rough edges (check inside the book as the inner pages may be shorter than the outer ones). Using an L-square, place your straight edge on the trimming mark at right angles to the spine. Holding your straight edge steady, begin to cut the pages one at a time, working from the folded spine to the foredge. Let the weight and sharpness of the blade do the work; your main job is to guide the knife and keep it at right angles to the edges it is cutting. When the head has been trimmed you should have a smooth edge at right angles to the spine. From the head, again using an L-square to guide your straight edge, trim the foredge and finally the tail, in both cases trimming to just inside the smallest page of the book. You should now have a neatly trimmed single-section book, which has a right angle at each corner (Fig 54).

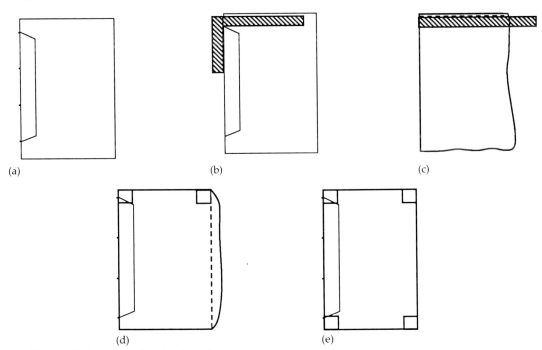

(a)   (b)   (c)

(d)   (e)

Fig 54   (a)–(e) Trimming the single section.

10. Cut your boards to fit your book. Your boards will have a square (the board that projects from the book at the head, tail and foredge) equal to their own thickness. In a single-section binding the spine of the book sticks out from the boards by ¼in (5mm). Mark this line along your book front and back with a pencil and ruler – this is the pitching line or guide line for measuring and sticking on your boards.

Length of boards = length of book + 2 board thicknesses.

Width of boards = width of book measured from the pitching line + 1 thickness of board.

To cut the length of your board, take the boards you have already prepared, which are square at all four corners, and proceed as follows:
(i) Set your dividers to the thickness of your board.
(ii) Mark the square at the head of your boards by making three prick marks.
(iii) Join up the prick marks using a ruler and sharp hard pencil.
(iv) Place the head of your book on the line you have just drawn, so that the desired square protrudes from the head of your book.
(v) Holding the book carefully in position, with a very sharp pencil or the tip of a scalpel, mark as accurately as you can where the tail of the book lies on the board with three dots.
(vi) Join up the dots using a ruler and pencil.
(vii) From this line mark your square – this is your cutting line.
11. Mark the desired width of your board by placing the long side of your board on the pitching line and marking

the foredge as you did with the head. From this line, mark your square and cut.

Remember, when you are using the board chopper, once the gauge is set you can cut any number of boards to the same length. Set the gauge and cut the lengths of both boards, then reset it and cut the widths. Check with your set square that all the corners of your boards are at right angles; if not . . . start again.
12. Attach the boards to the book, using glue for a quick bond. You will need a pile of clean waste paper, larger than your book, and you should also have a pair of pressing boards to hand.
(i) Make sure that your square is clearly marked on the inside of your boards, and that you have also marked the pitching line ¼in (5mm) in from the spine of your book.
(ii) Before glueing it is a good idea to work some glue into the brush, particularly if it has just been washed. This works out any excess water and helps to ensure an even covering of glue. Dip the end of the brush into the glue, and work the glue in on a piece of waste paper. Throw the glued paper away immediately.
(iii) Place the marked board on to a piece of waste paper with the markings facing you. With a moderate amount of glue on your brush (large dollops of glue or paste are to be avoided at all costs), and holding the board steady with the fingers of your left hand, work away from you, covering the board with a thin, even layer of glue.
(iv) When the board is glued, remove and throw away the glued waste paper and replace it immediately with a clean sheet – it will probably help to work on a pile of five or six sheets. Wipe around the edge of your board with a finger to remove any excess glue – this should render your square markings more visible, and

also means that when the book is pressed, and the glue forced to the edges by the pressure, there is less chance of glue oozing out and damaging the book or the pressing boards.

(v) With the glued board in front of you and the spine edge towards you, pick up your book (imagine it is a solid block rather than several pages) and carefully place it in position on the board, with your square projecting evenly at the head, tail and foredge. PVA glue does not dry immediately so there is time to readjust your book if you do not get it into position the first time.

(vi) When you are satisfied that the book is correctly positioned on the board, put a clean piece of waste paper inside the book, next to the newly glued board, and a piece of waste paper outside. Place the unglued board in position and protect it with waste paper, then put the whole between pressing boards. Place the sandwich of pressing boards, waste paper and book between the plates of your nipping press so that the screw of the press is in line with the centre point of the book – this will ensure as even a pressure as possible. Tighten the screw of the press so that the book is under a fairly hard pressure, and leave the book in the press for ten seconds. This short, sharp pressing is called 'nipping'.

(vii) Remove the book from the press, and take away the waste paper. Glue the second board and position the book as before – clean, dry waste must be put between each glued board and the book, and also on the outside between book and pressing boards. Nip. As you get more proficient you will be able to glue both boards before nipping.

(viii) Remove the book from the press and allow it to dry for at least three hours.

Do not worry if the boards curve inwards. This is caused by the pull of the board paper, and it will be counteracted by the covering material. The book should be dried standing up, with its boards open slightly, the foredge resting on a piece of board.

13. To cover your book with a half cloth cover (with the spine and corners of the book covered in cloth, and the rest of the board covered in decorative paper), proceed as follows. Cut one spine piece and four corners.

(i) To find the correct proportions of spine and corners, lay your book flat on the bench and measure a quarter of the width of the front of the book, from the foredge to the edge of the spine. Set your dividers to this distance and, measuring from the spine edge inwards, rule the line on the front board and then the back.

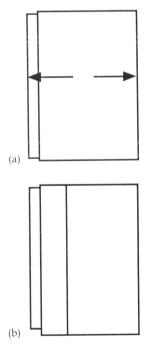

Fig 55 (a) and (b) Working out the correct measurement for the spine piece.

(ii)   Keep your dividers set to the same measurement ($\frac{1}{4}$ of the width of the book), and use your 45° set square to bisect the right angle of one of the corners of your book. With your dividers, measure from the corner along this line and mark. Complete the triangle by placing your set square on the mark at 90° to the bisecting line – you should now have an isosceles triangle whose perpendicular height is the same as the width of the spine piece when the book is lying closed on the bench. If you have a long, thin book you may find that a thinner spine piece and smaller corners look better. Conversely, on a square or landscape-shaped book, a wider spine with correspondingly larger corners looks better.

(iii)   When you have worked out the spine and corners of your book, cut a template for each out of heavy paper. For the spine template, wrap a strip of paper around the book from one spine piece mark to the other, to give you the correct width. The length is the length of your book boards plus 1in (2.5cm), to allow a turn-in of $\frac{1}{2}$in (1cm) at the head and tail. Cut a corner template allowing $\frac{1}{2}$in (1cm) turn-in on the two outer edges. The easiest way to make a corner template is to take the corner of your heavy paper, and mark a turning allowance of $\frac{1}{2}$in (1cm) along the two outside edges. Having marked the size of corner you need on your book board, place the paper inside the book with the two $\frac{1}{2}$in (1cm) turnings protruding. Mark the base line of your corner on your template, remove, draw the base line and cut. You should now have an accurate pattern of your corner with $\frac{1}{2}$in (1cm) turnings.

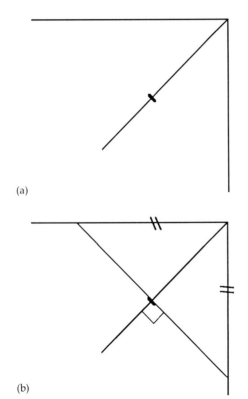

Fig 56   (a) and (b) Working out the correct measurements for the corners.

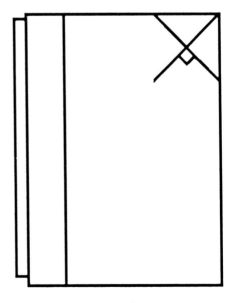

Fig 57   The spine and the corners drawn on the book.

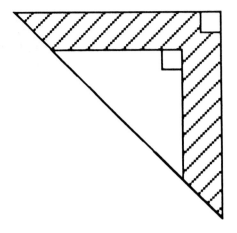

Fig 58   The pattern for the corner.

(iv)   Cloth, like machine-made paper and board, has a grain which runs parallel to the selvedge of the cloth. If you are in any doubt, cut off a small piece and tear it first one way and then the other. You will find that, like paper, cloth tears more easily with the grain than against it. The grain of the cloth should run from head to tail.

(v)   Place your templates on the cloth, draw around them, and cut out. Mark the ½in (1cm) turn-ins on all corners and the spine piece.

(vi)   Glue on the corners – plenty of waste paper must be to hand.

Carefully glue one corner, wiping away any excess glue from the edges. Place it on the book, adjusting it so that it is exactly in position with the ½in (1cm) turn-ins protruding from the boards.

Mitre the corner by placing your 45° set square to the corner of your board (*see* Fig 59(b)), rule along the line. Mark your cutting line by placing an offcut of your board against the 45° mitre line and drawing a second line, one board thickness away. To this line add $\frac{1}{32}$in. Cut.

Using your bone folder, carefully turn in the cloth along the head, taking care that you do not stretch it but firmly sticking it to the edge and to the inside of the board.

At the corner of your book you will have a tiny piece of cloth protruding from the end of the board. With your bone folder, tuck this piece down on to the foredge of the board. Do not pull it down too fiercely or you will make an ugly bulky corner.

Fold over the foredge turn-in, rubbing the cloth down firmly with your bone folder through a clean piece of waste paper, then glue on the remaining three corners in the same way.

A neat corner is very satisfying, and will also be stronger if there are no unsightly lumps (which could be rubbed or frayed), or little bits of board protruding.

(vii)   Cover the spine.

Glue the spine piece.

Lay the book (closed) on to the spine piece, so that the head and tail of the book are on the turn-in marks, and the long edge of the cloth is in line with the pitching line you have drawn on the front board.

Working through a sheet of clean waste paper, rub the cloth down firmly on to the board using the flat part of your bone folder.

Gently wrap the cloth over the spine, taking care that you do not stretch it. Position the cloth on the back board and rub it down.

Turn in the cloth at the head and tail by standing the book on its tail with the boards open. To avoid unnecessary damage, either to the book or the cloth, turn the loose turn-in on which the book is standing to the outside. Working with your bone folder, turn the cloth over to the inside of the boards at the head. Start

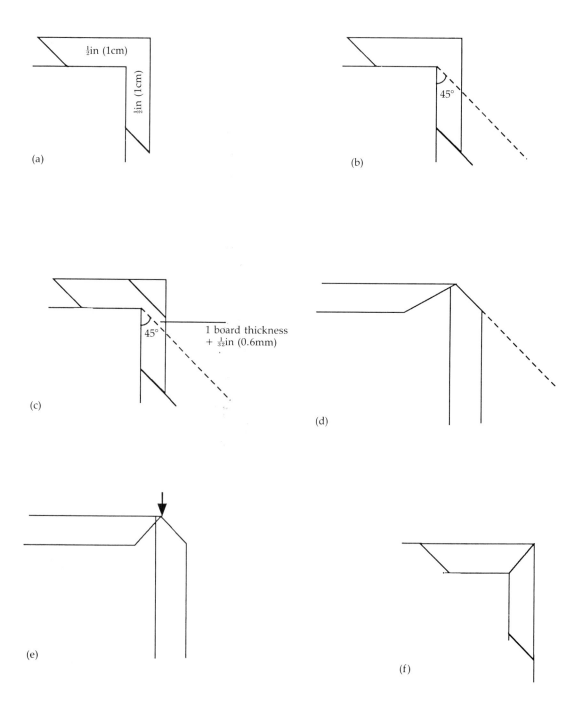

Fig 59   (a)–(f) Mitreing and glueing on the corner.

from the middle with the spine piece, holding the body of the book away, and fold the cloth over so that it lies between the book and the boards, making sure that the fold is level with the edge of the boards. Turn in the cloth on the boards. To finish the spine piece, lie the book on its spine and with your bone folder gently work around the head turn-in so that it is level and curves around the spine of the book. Repeat at the tail. Work along the whole length of your joint (the edge of the board parallel to the spine) with your bone folder, through a sheet of waste paper, front and back.

(viii)   Fill in with decorative paper.

Check that your corners and spine piece are accurate by measuring the sides of your corners with dividers – the board edges should be equal. If they are not, take the shortest measurement and trim so that all four corners are equal. Similarly, measure the width of your spine piece from the joint at the head and tail on the front and back boards; again, trim with a scalpel and straight edge to the shortest measurement.

When trimming on cloth make tiny marks with the points of your dividers, place your straight edge along the marks and cut. Do not rule a pencil line on the cloth.

Find the grain direction of your covering paper. (If you are using marbled paper you will probably have to trim off the very outer edges of your paper, as the pattern is usually less defined here.)

Having trimmed any waste, with a knife and straight edge cut two rectangles of paper (grain head to tail), the length of your book plus 1in (2.5cm) (to allow two $\frac{1}{2}$in (1cm) turn-ins), by the width of your book (measured from the edge of the cloth spine piece to the foredge) plus $\frac{1}{2}$in (1cm).

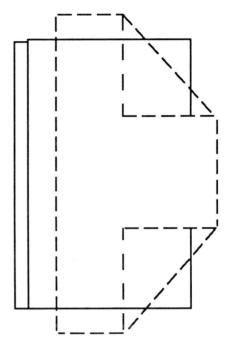

Fig 60   Cutting the decorative paper to size.

Mark your $\frac{1}{2}$in (1cm) turn-ins and also mark the head of each rectangle to ensure that the pattern is running the same way on the front and the back.

Place your front board paper in position, and gently crease the turn-ins so that the paper is bracketted in place around the book.

Holding the paper firmly in position, fold back first one corner and then the other along the diagonal cloth corner line. The paper should just overlap the cloth by $\frac{1}{32}$in. Take the paper off the book and cut off the paper at the corners with a scalpel and straight edge. Repeat with the back boards – do *not* assume that the two will be the same.

Glue the front board paper, wiping any excess glue from the edges. Position the paper so that it just covers the cloth by $\frac{1}{32}$in. Rub the paper down firmly with your bone folder through a sheet of waste paper, and turn in along the edges and on to the inside board.

14.   Put down the endpapers. Before doing this, check that all your turn-ins are

equal. If they are not, find the shortest measurement and, using dividers, scalpel and straight edge, mark and trim the cloth. Trim only on the board, do not try to trim the more vulnerable spine area.

(i)   You will need a pile of clean waste paper and two pressing boards. Lie the book flat on the bench with the front board open, place a clean piece of waste beneath the first page and, with a moderate amount of paste on your brush, paste the page, ensuring an even covering. Wipe excess paste from the edges and remove the paste-covered waste sheet.

(ii)   Making sure that the pasted paper does not curl over, close the board on to the book.

(iii)   Immediately insert a piece of dry waste between the damp, pasted board paper and the book.

(iv)   With protective waste papers on the pressing boards, place the book between the boards and nip.

(v)   Remove from press, change damp waste sheet.

(vi)   Repeat pasting operation on the back of the book. Nip.

(vii)   Remove from press and dry under a light weight, changing the waste sheets regularly so that they do not become damp.

Summary for single-section binding

1.   Find and mark grain of paper and board.
2.   Fold paper.
3.   Cut boards $\frac{1}{2}$in (1cm) longer, $\frac{1}{2}$in (1cm) wider.
4.   Mark up for sewing.
5.   Cut out mull, glue lightly to spine.
6.   Prick sewing holes.
7.   Sew.
8.   Trim.
9.   Cut the boards to size.
10.   Glue the boards to the book.
11.   Cover.
12.   Put down the endpapers.
13.   Dry.

BINDING A SINGLE-SECTION PAMPHLET

Most of the operations for binding a pamphlet are exactly the same as for your single section.

1.   Look carefully at your pamphlet and decide whether you are going to discard the cover or bind it in.
2.   If you are going to bind in the cover: check that the spine of the pamphlet is not worn along the fold; if it is, it will need to be strengthened.
3.   Open the pamphlet and undo any staples that may be holding it together, remove and throw them away. If the pamphlet has been sewn, cut the thread and pull it out of the holes.
4.   If the pamphlet spine needs strengthening, with a scalpel and straight edge cut a strip of repair tissue (Kozushi is a good strength), about $\frac{1}{4}$in (5mm) wide – it should overlap the spine or section to be strengthened by $\frac{1}{8}$in (2.5mm) on each side – by the length of the section plus $\frac{1}{2}$in (1cm). The repairing of backs of sections like this is called 'guarding', and the strips of repair tissue are called 'guards'.

(i)   Place the guard on a piece of waste paper and paste it.

(ii)   Place the section on the guard so that the bolt or fold of the section lies along the centre of the guard and fold the guard around the section.

(iii)   Allow the guard to dry and trim off

any excess at the head and tail.

5.   In single-section books you use the two outer sheets of the book to attach it to the boards. Naturally, if you used the two outer pages of your pamphlet in this way, you would lose an important part of the text, so you have to provide the necessary extra pages. You will need to cut three pieces of paper which will wrap around the outside of your pamphlet. The outer one will be glued to the board, the second one will be the paste down, and the third will serve as a free endpaper, or fly leaf, to be a partner to the paste down and introduce the reader to the book. The outer sheet, which is not seen when the book is finished, can be of cartridge paper, while the other two can be coloured to suit the colour scheme of the pamphlet – an Ingres is suitable for this. Cut your three extra folios so that they are ½in (1cm) longer and ½in (1cm) wider than the pamphlet when folded around it. Wrap around the pamphlet, knocking it level to the head.

6.   Cut a pair of boards ½in (1cm) longer and ½in (1cm) wider, as before.

7.   Mark up for sewing. A problem might occur where your new sewing marks are very close to the old holes which are already there. In this case, use the old holes, as new ones would weaken rather than strengthen the book. Remember also that you have an extra ½in (1cm) of paper at the tail which must be accounted for when measuring for sewing as it will later be trimmed to fit the book.

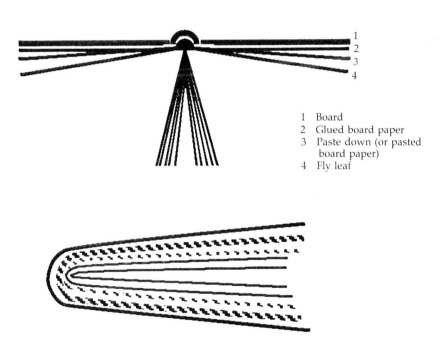

1 Board
2 Glued board paper
3 Paste down (or pasted
   board paper)
4 Fly leaf

Fig 61   Single section, showing the boards and endpapers.

8. Cut and lightly glue mull.

9. Prick sewing holes. Sew.

10. Trim the endpapers to fit the book, using a knife and straight edge, and placing the book on a piece of cutting board. When trimming the foredge keep the book closed, place the straight edge between the book and the endpaper and cut, one sheet at a time, first at the front and then, turning the book over, at the back.

11. Cut the boards to size, and glue and attach them.

12. Cover the pamphlet. A full cloth cover uses the same techniques for covering as the half cloth.

(i) Make a template for the cloth by placing the pamphlet (closed) on a sheet of paper. Draw around the board, then turn the pamphlet over and draw around the second board. Add $\frac{1}{2}$in (1cm) turn-in allowance all round.

(ii) Cut the cloth out and mark turn-ins.

(iii) Glue the cloth, placing it on waste paper.

(iv) Lay the closed pamphlet on the cloth, and rub the cloth down on to the board with the flat curved side of your bone folder (do this through waste paper).

(v) Fold the cloth over the spine and on to the second board.

(vi) Mitre the corners.

(vii) Then turn in at the head. This is exactly the same as for the half cloth binding, the only difference being that you have a longer strip of cloth to deal with.

(viii) Turn in at the tail.

(ix) Turn in one foredge and then the other, taking care to form neat corners as you do so. Sharpen up the turn-ins, and work on the spine turn-ins and joints as before.

13. Check the turn-ins and trim if necessary. Paste down the endpapers. Nip. Allow to dry.

6 Flat-Back Binding

A flat-back book is exactly as its name implies – with a flat back or spine instead of a rounded one. Although this method of binding is not particularly strong, it is suitable for slim books, particularly paper backs, and can give a much loved book an extra few years of reading life.

SEWN FLAT-BACK BINDING

Prepare your working area. As before, make sure that all bench surfaces are clean and covered with large sheets of waste paper. Make sure that all your tools, equipment and materials are to hand.

1. Collate. Before you do anything to your book check through it carefully to see: that all the pages are there; that all the illustrations are there – if they are loose, ensure that they are all in the correct place and facing the right way; whether any pages are in need of repair.

2. Cut two pairs of boards (four in all) each ½in (1cm) longer and ½in (1cm) wider than your book. One pair will be your book boards and the other pair will be 'rough' boards, used to handle the book and to protect it throughout the working operations or forwarding (in large binderies the books were 'forwarded', sent forward eventually to the tooling department, where they were finished). Do not underestimate the importance of cutting *both* pairs of boards square.

3. Pull the book apart. This operation is known as 'pulling' and should be done very carefully as much unnecessary damage can be done to the book at this stage.

(i)   Carefully remove the cover.

(ii) Remove the old spine linings and glue, by placing the book between rough boards in the lying press, having knocked it level to the spine first – the book should be held firmly, with about 2in (5cm) of the book (protected by rough boards) protruding.

(iii) With a penknife, scrape off as much

Tools	Equipment	Materials
Pencil	Weight ½lb/200g	Waste paper
Dividers	Lying press	Cloth
Needle	Nipping press	Mull
Straight edge	Hammer	Board ⅛in thick
Bone folder	Two pressing boards	Glue
Drawing pins	Knocking down iron	Tape
Set square		Paper for endpapers
Sharp knife or scalpel		Paste
Glue and paste brushes		3-strand thread

of the old lining, paper, mull and glue as you can, being careful that you do not damage the actual spine of the book.

(iv)   If you cannot clean the spine completely like this then apply a thin layer of paste and leave for about 10 minutes. The action of the paste on the glue will be intensified if a thin piece of polythene is placed over the pasted spine. When the paste has softened the glue, clean it off, repeating the pasting if necessary.

Unfortunately, not all modern glues used in commercially-produced books are soluble in water and sometimes it will be better for the paper of the book to be pulled from the glue, after the sewing has been cut. With such books the glue from the spine usually remains intact as a strip, but they are the exception and most glues will soften with paste.

(v)   When the spine is clean, remove the book from the press. Find the middle of the first section, and cut each sewing stitch with a scalpel, being careful not to cut the paper as well as the thread. When the stitches are undone, find the last page of the section – the signatures marking the beginning of each section will be useful – and gently pull the section away from the book.

4.   Guard any sections that are damaged using Kozushi paper. As with the single section, the guards should overlap the sections by not more than $\frac{1}{8}$in (2.5mm).

(i)   Cut the required number of strips, making them $\frac{1}{2}$in (1cm) longer than necessary.

(ii)   Paste each strip, place the section to be guarded in the middle of the guard, and wrap the guard around the section.

(iii)   Allow the guards to dry, and then trim. When drying the guards, place the sections spine to foredge with the guarded portions protruding – this way

the guards will dry naturally, and the book will stay in the correct order. When guarding you are adding to the thickness or swell of the spine. If you have to guard several sections at the front of the book it is advisable to guard a similar number of sections at the back, or a lopsided book will result. This problem does not often arise but it is worth bearing in mind. Also, the first two and the last two sections of a book should always be guarded for strength, as these sections take more wear and tear than the others.

5.   Cut a pair of endpapers. The simplest form of endpaper is a single folded piece of paper which is held in place by a strip of paste at the spine edge. These are called 'tipped-on endpapers' and are frequently used in commercial binding. However, they are not particularly strong, so we will begin with a simple sewn-on endpaper.

(i)   Choose a paper that matches that of your book in colour, weight and texture as closely as possible.

(ii)   Check the grain – remember it should run from head to tail.

(iii)   Cut four pieces of paper which, when folded, will be $\frac{1}{2}$in (1cm) longer and $\frac{1}{2}$in (1cm) wider than your book.

(iv)   Place one folded sheet inside another so that you have two pairs of endpapers, each one consisting of two folded sheets of paper.

(v)   Make sure that your endpapers are cut square.

6.   Mark the book up for sewing.

(i)   Place the endpapers in position at the beginning and end of the book, and mark the head with pencil.

(ii)   With the book between your rough boards, knock it level at the spine and the head – the importance of square boards will be apparent here as you are beginning to form the eventual shape of the book.

Tap it gently on the bench, allowing the sections to drop into position.

(iii) When the sections are level, and the head and spine of the book square, place it (still between rough boards) in a lying press, holding it firmly in the middle of the press with about 1in (2.5cm) of spine protruding.

(iv) Using dividers, ruler, pencil and L-square, mark the spine clearly for sewing. For strength a minimum of four ½in (1cm) tapes is desirable, although, as with everything in bookbinding, the final decision depends upon the book. For a normal paperback four or five tapes should be adequate.

(v) Using your dividers mark ½in (1cm) from the head and ¾in (1.5cm) up from the tail. If you make the point mark on the rough board edge, then rule the lines using an L-square, you will avoid damaging the sections. This line is the kettle stitch (from the German word 'Ketteln', meaning a catch stitch). The slightly higher tail kettle stitch will account for any discrepancy in the length of the sections.

(vi) If you have decided on four tapes, measure the distance between the kettle stitches and divide it by five. Set your dividers to this distance, divide the space between the kettle stitches into equal parts and draw faint pencil lines across the spine, using your L-square to guide you. You should have four equally spaced lines in addition to your two kettle stitches. These lines mark the mid-points of your tape marks. Using dividers set to half the tape width mark, rule a line on each side of the mid-points. These are the actual sewing guides for your tapes. If the original sewing marks are close to the ones you are making, make use of them. (Fig 62.)

7. Saw the cerf.

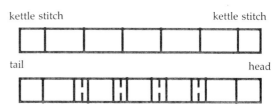

Fig 62   Marking up for sewing on tapes.

(i) Take the book out of the press and remove the endpapers, which are never sawn. Mark which is the front and back endpaper and put them carefully to one side.

(ii) Replace the book, minus endpapers, between its rough boards, knock level to the spine and head and put into the press as before.

(iii) With a fine saw gently saw along the kettle stitch lines at the head and tail, holding the book steady and the sections together with your left hand. The resulting indentation or 'cerf' need not be huge, just enough to accommodate the kettle stitch.

(iv) Remove the book from the press and reunite it with its endpapers.

8. Sew on the tapes. A sewing frame is not necessary for this; all you need is a pressing board and drawing pins.

(i) Cut your tapes the width of the spine of your book plus 2½in (6cm). The tapes should overlap the sides of the book by 1in (2.5cm), the extra ½in (1cm) allowing for swell and accidents.

(ii) Lie the book on the pressing board with the spine to a long edge, the head to your right. Pin the tapes in position, lining them up with the tape marks on the spine of the book. Remove the book from the board.

(iii) Thread the needle. It is a good idea to prick the sewing holes in the endpapers before sewing, thus making sure that you are going directly through the centre of the fold.

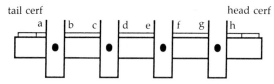

Fig 63   Tapes pinned in position.

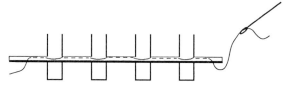

Fig 64   Sewing.

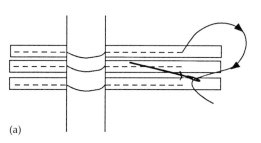

(a)

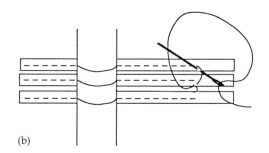

(b)

Fig 65   (a) and (b) Sewing the kettle stitch.

(iv)   Placing the front endpaper in position on the pressing board, and holding the folded sheets open with your left hand, insert the needle at the tail cerf, pulling the thread through until an end of 2in (5cm) is left on the outside. Receiving the needle in your left hand, pass it out to your right through hole A. Continue as follows, passing the needle from hand to hand:

Back into the section round the tape at b.
Out at c.
Back into the section round the tape at d.
Out at e.
Back into the section round the tape at f.
Out at g.
Back into the section round the tape at h.
And finally out at the head cerf.

(v)   Take the first section, knock it level to the head. Holding it open in the middle with your left hand, place the section on top of the endpaper with the heads level. Insert your needle at the head cerf and work down the section, sewing around

the tapes as before to the tail.

(vi)   When you reach the tail, tie the two loose ends of thread together using a reef knot.

(vii)   Take the second section and sew as above, starting from the tail. At the head you will link the first and second sections with a kettle stitch. When your needle emerges at the head, pass it between the two lower sections, catching the linking stitch as you do so. Pass the needle through the resulting loop in the thread and tighten gently, making sure that the kettle stitch now formed lies in the sawn cerf.

(viii)   Continue until all the sections are sewn, checking that their order is correct by the signature, and that they are level at the head. Should you need to renew your thread, either start the next section with a new thread and join the two new ends at the kettle stitch with a reef knot after you have sewn the section, or join the two threads inside the section using a weaver's knot (see page 151).

(ix)   When the last section is sewn finish with a double kettle stitch for extra strength. Instead of cutting the thread off to ½in (1cm) immediately after completing the kettle stitch, it can be passed down and round the kettle stitches for a few sections before being cut off.

(x)   Rub the spine down with a bone folder to close the sewing holes. Make sure that all knots lie in the cerf and that the finished spine is as neat and smooth as possible.

9.   Knock out the swell. You will find that the spine of your book will now be wider than it was, not only because of the additional thickness of the thread, but also because you will have introduced more air into the sections by opening them up. The importance of swell will be discussed later. For your flat back you need to reduce the swell and consolidate the book.

(i)   Place the book between its rough boards with the tapes outside (this is to avoid damaging the paper). Knock the book level at the head and spine. It is important that all the sections are level and that the spine is flat.

(ii)   Place the book in the lying press allowing 2in (5cm) of the book to protrude from the press.

(iii)   Stand at the end of your lying press with your knocking down iron in your left hand and your hammer in your right. Place the knocking down iron so that it lies against the left-hand side of your

Fig 66   Knocking out the swell.

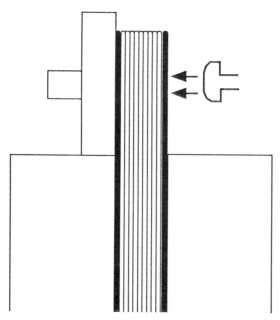

Fig 67   Knocking out the swell.

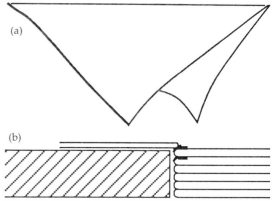

Fig 68   (a) and (b) Pasting up the first two and last two sections.

book, and hammer the right-hand side of the book. You will see as the swell is reduced the tapes buckle across the spine of the book. When this happens, pull them straight – take great care not to pull them out altogether, as replacing a tape is a tedious business.

10.   Paste up the first two and last two sections – these four sections take most of the stresses and strains.

(i)   Open the book between the first and second sections so that the first section and the endpapers are opened flat on the bench.

(ii)   Take a piece of waste paper and fold it across the grain to give you a long, straight edge from which to work.

(iii)   Measure $\frac{1}{8}$in (2.5mm) in from the spine edge of the second section, place your folded waste on this line and with a small brush paste away from the waste.

(iv)   Close the first section on to the

second and repeat with the first section and the endpapers.

(v)   While the paste is still damp, knock the sections level at the head and spine.

(vi)   Repeat with the last two sections, and allow to dry.

11.   Trim your endpapers. Lie the book on a piece of board, and place the straight edge under the book but on top of the endpaper, level with the edge of the text. Trim. Turn the book over and repeat at the front and at the tails.

12.   Line the spine.

(i)   Place the book in the lying press between rough boards with the tapes inside (having knocked the book level at the head and spine as a matter of course).

(ii)   Cut a piece of mull to overlap the spine of your book by 1in (2.5cm) on each side – the width of your spine plus 2in (5cm). In length it should cover the head and tail kettle stitches, ending half-way between the kettle stitches and the head and tail of the book.

(iii)   Glue the spine. Although you want the spine to be thoroughly glued, do not flood it on to the book. Spare glue can cause damage. Rub the glue well into the spine between the sections with your fingers.

(iv) Place the mull on the glued spine and rub it down firmly.

(v) Take the book out of the press and cut the mull inside the rough boards. Replace the book in the press.

(vi) Glue the spine a second time and line it with Kraft paper to cover the length and width of the spine exactly. Although it is possible to measure the spine and to cut a piece of paper to fit, as always it is easier to work from the book.

Take a piece of Kraft paper, $\frac{1}{2}$in (1cm) longer and at least $\frac{1}{2}$in (1cm) wider than the spine, with the grain running from head to tail. Make sure that one long edge of the paper is straight and at right angles to the head.

Place the known straight edge and right angle to the back edge and head of the spine.

Rub the paper down thoroughly.

Trim the excess paper by folding it back, creasing and trimming it with a penknife – a scalpel can be too sharp for this sort of work – along the long edge. The tail too can be trimmed in this way, or with scissors when the book has been taken out of the press.

Large books may need a second or even a third spine lining, but avoid unnecessary lining as too many can make the book difficult to open.

Remove the book from the press.

13. Cut the boards and spine piece to fit. Your square should be equal to one board thickness all round, so the length of your boards will be the length of your book plus two board thicknesses (for measuring and cutting details *see* page 60). The width of your boards will be the width of your book from spine to foredge. When the boards are correctly positioned on the book, with the square at head, tail and foredge, the boards will be moved one thickness away from the spine of the book, to allow a space for the boards to turn or hinge on. This will create a gap or groove between the spine piece and the board, called a 'French groove', and also give you your correct square on the foredge. In brief, the length should equal the length of the book plus two board thicknesses, while the width should equal the width of the book.

You will also need a spine piece the length of the board by the width of the spine plus the thickness of two boards (measured when the boards are in position one board thickness away from the spine). It is important that the spine measurements be taken with the boards in this position as the slight swell of the spine will take up part of the board thickness. The spine piece is made from board, and if you use a slightly thinner type it gives a more elegant appearance. Find your spine measurement using your dividers.

14. Mark and cut out the cloth.

(i) Rule one long straight line across the grain to this measure and rule a second parallel line $\frac{3}{4}$in (15mm) away from it. On this line place one board of your book and draw round it.

(ii) The spine piece lies between the two boards and the gap between the spine piece and the board must be correct – sufficient to allow the cloth to cover the following distance: down one board thickness, across the joint, up a second board thickness and along the spine board edge. It is therefore three board thicknesses, plus the thickness of the spine board. The most accurate way of marking this is to make a little jig of the required numbers and thicknesses of

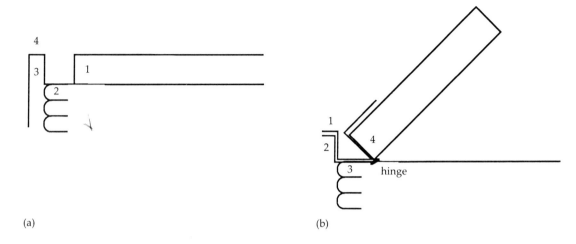

Fig 69   (a) and (b) Distance of board from the spine piece.

board. Mark the groove, place the spine piece in position and mark it. Mark the second groove and the second board.

(iii)   Mark ¾in (15mm) turn-in all round. Cut out the cloth. (Fig 69.)

15.   Glue the cloth and make the case.

(i)   With lots of clean waste paper to work on, glue the cloth.

(ii)   Place the boards and spine stiffener in position.

(iii)   Turn the whole case over and, working through clean waste paper, rub the cloth down firmly with your fist and then your bone folder, taking care that you do not stretch the cloth. Remove and throw away the glued waste.

(iv)   Mitre the corners (see page 64).

(v)   Turn in the cloth at the head, and at the tail, then turn in the cloth on the foredges and make the corners.

(vi)   Turning the case over, work along the joints with your bone folder (through a piece of waste in order to avoid marking the cloth).

16.   Check that the turn-ins are even. If not, trim to the smallest one after the cloth has dried.

17.   Cased bindings are most usually lettered before the books are cased (see pages 114–115).

18.   Case the book in.

(i)   Make discreet marks with your dividers to show where your squares are at the head, tail and foredge.

(ii)   Place one waste sheet beneath the front board paper, and paste, including under the mull and tapes. Wipe away the excess paste from the edges of the page, and remove the waste sheet.

(iii)   Making sure that the pasted page is not curled over, and holding the book as a solid block, carefully place it in position on the board, checking that all three squares are equal. If not, the paste will allow for readjustment, as long as you are careful.

(iv)   When the book is in position, nip, placing clean dry waste inside and outside at the front and back. Although at this stage only one endpaper is pasted down, wrap the case around the book and position the book correctly before placing between pressing boards. The edge of the pressing boards should come to the edge of the book boards, and the spine should be free. If the spine is pressed, particularly with a flat back, you will certainly damage it.

(v)   Having nipped the first endpaper for 10 seconds, remove from the press and paste the second endpaper. Paste does not dry as quickly as glue, so treat your newly-pasted-down endpaper with respect. As before, treat your book as though it were a solid block. Do not try to put the endpaper down on its own as a single sheet, and lay the book in position on the second board. Nip with new waste sheets inside and out, front and back.

19.   Remove the book from the press, replace waste sheets with dry ones and leave your book to dry under a light weight for one to two hours, replacing the waste sheets regularly. Then allow it to dry naturally with the boards slightly open and the foredge supported.

Summary for flat-back binding

1.   Collate.
2.   Cut boards.
3.   Clean off spine.
4.   Pull.
5.   Guard.
6.   Cut endpapers.
7.   Mark up for sewing.
8.   Remove endpapers and saw cerf.
9.   Sew.
10.   Knock out swell.
11.   Paste up first and last two sections.
12.   Trim endpapers.
13.   Line the spine.
14.   Cut the boards and spine piece.
15.   Cut the cloth.
16.   Make the case.
17.   Letter the case.
18.   Paste down endpapers.

FLAT-BACK BINDING OF AN UNSEWN PAPERBACK

William Hancock's caoutchouc binding, in which single leaves were roughened and bound together by a rubber-based adhesive, must have seemed a blessing in 1836. It speeded up forwarding considerably, bypassing marking up, sawing and sewing, but still giving a flexible spine. Unfortunately he did not realise that the rubber-based glue would eventually perish, leaving future readers with a handful of loose sheets. The 'perfect binding' (as it was called) is still used today, usually for cheaply-produced books and paperbacks. Plastic-based glues are now used, but the binding method remains unsatisfactory and all too often the reader is still left in a sea of flying pages. Although 'perfect-bound' books can be reglued, this method can really only be regarded as a temporary measure, and a stronger and more permanent form of binding can be achieved by over-sewing.

1.   Collate.
2.   Cut boards.
3.   Remove the cover from your paperback. If you want to include the front cover and possibly the title (perhaps if you are working at home with no access to finishing tools) in your binding, put them to one side.
4.   Clean off the spine. Sometimes the glue used for perfect bindings is very strong and is not easily soluble in water – in these cases, carefully take a few pages at a time and pull the pages gently from the glue.
5.   Cut endpapers as before.
6.   Knock the book level to the spine and head.
7.   Place the book in the lying press and

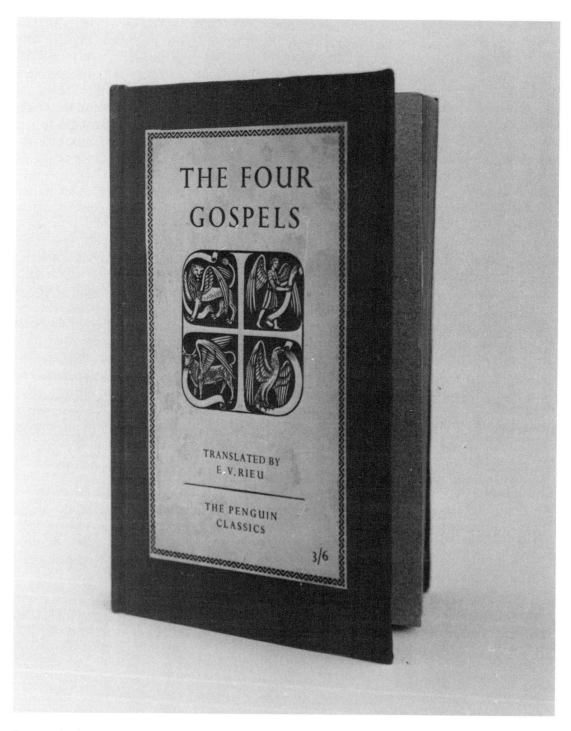

Fig 70   Flat-back book with inset cover, bound by one of the author's students.

mark up for sewing. It is not necessary to saw the cerf.

8.   While the book is still held firmly in the press, glue the spine lightly, rubbing the glue well in. This will hold your pages together while you are sewing them.

9.   Set up your tapes for sewing.

10.   Decide how many pages you are going to have per section – six or eight is the usual number, depending on the thickness of the paper and, to some extent, the size of the book. Although large sections will mean less sewing for you they can be bulky and difficult to sew. Once you have decided how many pages you are going to have in each section, work out from the number of pages in the book how many, if any, pages will be left over. These remaining pages should be divided equally between the first and the last sections. For example, if you are sewing a book of 164 pages into sections of eight, you will have 20 sections with four pages remaining. You could either sew a small section at the back of the book with four pages, or sew the first two and the last two sections with nine pages, which would distribute any extra swell evenly. If your book has 167 pages, the best way of dealing with the additional seven would be to sew a seven-page section at the end, the lack of one page making little difference to the balance of the book. If your book contains some pages that are thicker than others (this sometimes happens with illustrations), the easiest solution is to let each one of these pages count for two normal pages.

11.   (i)   Count and pull your first 'section' from the book – the slight glueing of the spine will now become apparent.

(ii)   Measure ⅒in (2.5mm) (not more) in from the spine edge and rule a very faint line. As you become more used to over-sewing it will not always be necessary to mark the over-sewing line, but it is a good idea to start with.

(iii)   Although the positions of your tapes and kettle stitches are marked on the spine of your book, you will find it helpful to make tiny marks on the uppermost page along the sewing line to show you exactly where they are going to be. (Fig 71.)

(iv)   With your first section or gathering marked up you are ready to start over-sewing. To make life easier to begin with, make your needle holes first, pricking the holes for the kettle stitches and the tapes, and also one hole in between each tape and between the first and last tape and the kettle stitch. (Fig 71.)

(v)   Using thin 2-strand thread (sometimes called over-sewing thread) sew the first endpapers as normal, starting at the tail.

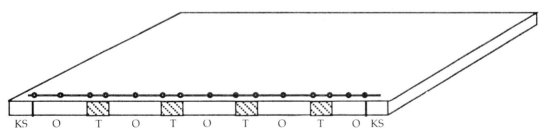

KS   O   T   O   T   O   T   O   T   O   KS

Fig 71

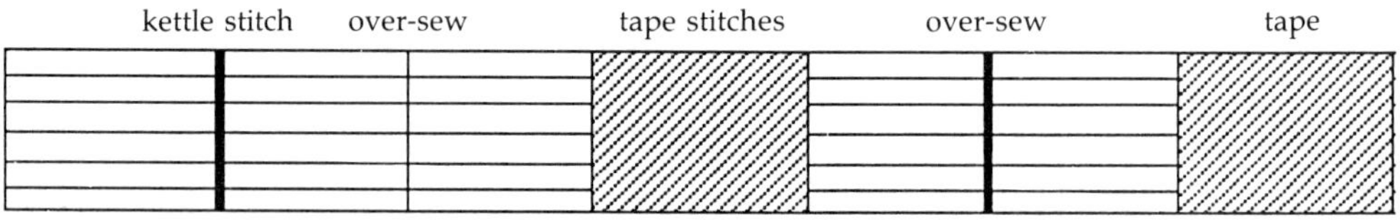

Fig. 72   Much enlarged diagram of part of section.

right

wrong

Fig 73

Fig 74

(vi)   Place your first section on top of the endpaper, head to the right, spine edge towards you and the first page face downwards on the endpaper.

(vii)   Move the section slightly towards you to facilitate the over-sewing. When over-sewing it is important to make sure that your needle is inserted absolutely vertically, or the last couple of pages in the section will either be missed or not sewn securely. (*See* Figs 73 and 74.)

(viii)   Insert your needle downwards at the head kettle stitch, lining the head up with the head of the endpapers. Pull the thread through and secure the two together with a kettle stitch.

The next stitch is an oversewn stitch; the needle is passed downwards through the section between the kettle stitch and the tape on the over-sewing line $\frac{1}{8}$in (2.5mm) from the spine.

The tape stitches are formed by making a blanket stitch. The needle is inserted downwards at 'a' and the thread pulled through. The needle and thread is then passed up through the loosely formed stitch and gently pulled tight. Pass the thread around the tape and down through the second tape hole. This time, instead of passing the thread directly back up through the loop formed, twist the loop to your left and pass the needle up through the loop, gently pulling tight so that the tape is now secure. (*See* Figs 75–79.) Continue as follows:

Over-sew.
Tape stitches.
Over-sew.
Tape stitches.
Over-sew.
Tape stitches.
Over-sew, then kettle stitch.

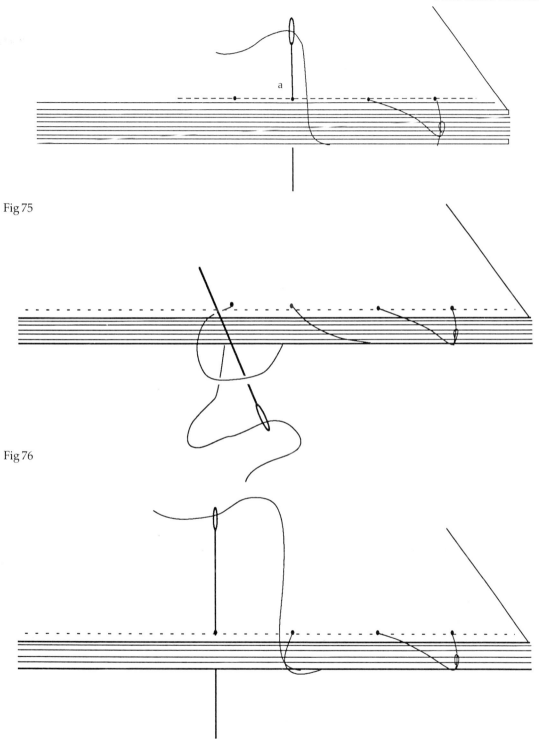

a

Fig 75

Fig 76

Fig 77

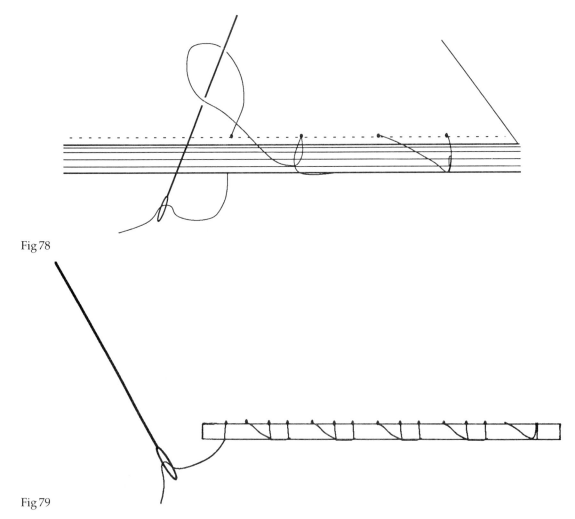

Fig 78

Fig 79

Close the holes made by sewing by rub-bing down with a bone folder through waste paper, after each section is sewn.
(ix) As with sewing on tapes, join the two loose ends or thread with a reef knot and start on the second section, sewing in exactly the same way as the first. Swing the section slightly towards you and use the kettle stitch as a hinge to make sewing easier and to ensure that the needle is inserted vertically. When you reach the end of the section, link it to the preceding sections with a kettle stitch as normal.

(x) When a new length of thread is needed, either join in mid-section with a weaver's knot or start from the beginning of the section as usual, simply knotting the two ends together.

It is possible to over-sew each section separately and then thread the tapes through afterwards, but this method seems to result in a very loose book. The kettle stitches have to be made by knot-ting all the loose ends, which also adds bulk, and this is less secure than the properly-formed kettle stitch.

12. Knock out the swell.
13. Paste up first two and last two sections.
14. Trim endpapers.
15. Glue and line the spine.
16. Cut boards and spine piece. If you are going to include part of the original cover in the binding, a frame of manilla is made at this point. To do this, proceed as follows:

(i) Cut out the part of the cover you are going to use with a scalpel and straight edge.

(ii) Place the front board on the book with the correct groove between the board edge and the spine piece (which should also be in position) – this is to allow you to find the true centre.

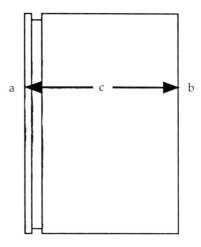

Fig 80   Position of board.

Fig 81   Set of books with inset covers by a student.

(iii)   Measure from a to b to find the mid-point c. Find and mark half the width of your cover, and line it up with point c on the board.

(iv)   Your cover inset should be slightly higher than the true horizontal mid-point of the book, and you will be left with a frame around your inset. This area is to be filled with manilla, so that when the book is covered the inset will sit inside the frame, and not only present a neater face to the world but also be less vulnerable.

(v)   To cut the frame, draw around your accurately placed inset – this will give you the exact widths needed for the sides of the frame. Measure the width with dividers, and using a knife and straight edge cut the strips of manilla. Glue the manilla to the board, butting the edges together. Nip.

17.   Cut the cloth and cover the case as before. Work the cloth into the frame with your bone folder.

18.   Paste down the endpapers.

19.   Glue the inset, wiping any excess glue from the edges, and place it in the frame. Rub down firmly.

20.   Nip, placing a piece of lining fabric (terylene or acetate) between the outer board and the protective waste paper. This will avoid any danger of the inset cover sticking to the waste paper should any glue accidentally ooze out.

21.   Allow to dry under a light weight, constantly changing the waste sheets.

The same technique can be used with spine pieces on flat-back bindings. Again, position the inset piece slightly up of the horizontal centre line.

If the piece to be inset is considerably smaller than the board of the book, cut a piece of manilla the size of the board. Find the vertical centre of the whole book (*see* page 83), and position the inset piece, marking its place exactly. Working on a large piece of rough board, and using a scalpel and straight edge, cut out the window. Glue the manilla to the board and proceed as before.

7 Cased Books

Although the flat-back method offers some protection for paperbacks and slim volumes, it is not suitable for heavier books. After some time the sections will tend to fall forward, putting strain on the joints. To prevent this happening larger and better quality books are 'rounded', giving the book a rounded spine with a corresponding curved foredge, and then 'backed' – the sections are hammered over each other, so that they support each other, retaining the round.

1. Prepare work surface.
2. Collate.
3. Find the grain of the boards and the paper. Cut four boards, $\frac{1}{2}$in (1cm) longer and $\frac{1}{2}$in (1cm) wider than your book.
4. Cut and make your endpapers. Although folded endpapers or tipped-on endpapers are often used for cased bindings, a different style, called a 'made endpaper', can also be used. These endpapers should be made at least 24 hours before you start to sew your book, as they must be allowed to dry.

You will need waste paper, paste, a paste brush, four pressing boards, and four folded pieces of 'white' paper and two folded pieces of coloured paper, both cut to the same size – $\frac{1}{2}$in (1cm) wider and $\frac{1}{2}$in (1cm) longer than the book when folded.

When choosing the paper, try to match the white paper with that of the book in colour, weight and texture. The coloured paper should tone in with the cloth to be used and should be the same weight as the white paper if possible.

(i) Take one folded white piece of paper and one folded colour. Place a sheet of waste inside the folded white and paste the outside sheet (Fig 82).

(ii) Remove the waste, and place the folded colour on to the pasted white, making sure that the folds are exactly together (Fig 83).

Hand tools	Equipment	Materials
Pencil	Pressing boards	Waste paper
Bone folder	Nipping press	Mull
Scissors	Backing boards	Thread
Dividers	Weight	Glue and paste
Needle	Lying press	Board
Scalpel	Knocking down iron	Kraft paper
Straight edge		Tape
Glue and paste brushes		Manila
		Cloth
		Guarding paper
		Paper for endpapers – two sheets of white, one sheet coloured

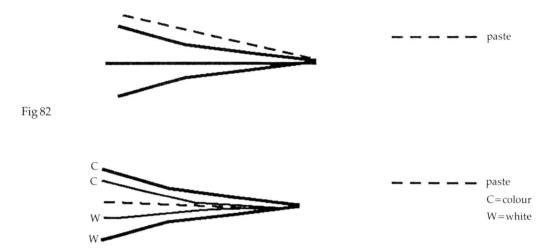

- - - - - paste

Fig 82

C
C

- - - - - paste
C=colour
W
W=white
W

Fig 83

(iii) Place dry clean waste each side of the pasted 'made' sheet and protective waste sheets outside, place between pressing boards and nip.

(iv) Remove the endpaper from the press and take the second folded white. Paste ⅛in (2.5mm) from the folded edge of the first folded white and tip the second folded white on to it (folded edge to folded edge) – this is called 'tipping on'. (Fig 84.) Rub down firmly with your bone folder through waste.

(v) Fold the outside white sheet around the whole endpaper. Again, rub down with bone folder. The endpaper can be hung on a line to dry, and then after half an hour placed under a light weight with clean dry waste outside and each side of the made sheet. (Note that when drying, the waste sheets should be replaced regularly as they become damp.) Repeat the process with the second endpaper.

The endpapers consist of one waste sheet, one board paper, one made sheet and two fly leaves. The waste sheet protects the endpaper while the book is being forwarded, but is removed before the book is cased in. The made sheet is formed to avoid the rather unattractive occurrence of a coloured sheet and a white sheet being opposite each other. It was also developed to hide the sometimes imperfect or stained backs of marbled papers.

5. Pull the book.

(i) Assuming you are not going to keep the old cover or the endpapers, open the front board and with a sharp knife cut through the fold of the endpapers, the old mull and tapes, taking care not to damage the book itself. Repeat at the back, so that the book is now free from its case.

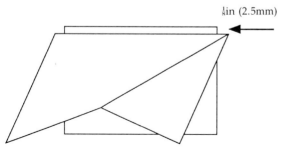

⅛in (2.5mm)

Fig 84   'Tipping on' endpapers.

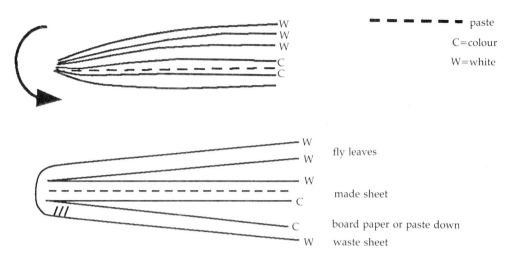

paste

C=colour

W=white

W fly leaves

made sheet

board paper or paste down

waste sheet

Fig 85 (a) and (b) Made endpapers.

(ii) Clean off the spine. Place the book between rough boards in the lying press, and remove as much of the old spine linings as you can. If you are unable to clean the spine completely like this, paste it lightly, cover with a thin sheet of polythene and leave for about 10 minutes before returning to the job.

(iii) When the spine is clean, pull the book apart by cutting the sewing threads in the middle of each section.

6. Knock out the old joint. If the book has already been rounded and backed, you will notice that the old joint is still present. This must be hammered out so that the sections are once more flat.

(i) Place the knocking down iron in one end of the lying press, and close the press so that the iron is held firmly.

(ii) Fold a piece of waste paper across the grain and place the first section inside, fold to fold.

(iii) Place section inside its protective piece of paper on the knocking down iron.

(iv) Hammer along the joint, thus hammering it out, so that you end up with a flat section.

(v) Continue until all the sections are flat.

7. Guard any damaged sections.

8. Making sure that the heads of your endpapers are square, place the book with endpapers in position (waste sheets to the outside) between rough boards, knocked level to the head and spine, in the lying press and mark up for sewing as described (see page 71). Remember to remove the endpapers before sawing the cerf.

9. Set up tapes for sewing. Sew through the folded white of the endpaper, and then sew the rest of the book as described on pages 71–72.

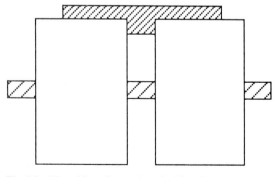

Fig 86 Knocking down iron held in lying press.

Fig 87   Rounding.

10.   Knock out the excess swell.

11.   Paste up the first two and last two sections, and allow to dry.

12.   Place the book (between rough boards, knocked level to the head and spine) in the press for glueing. Glue carefully between the tapes, rubbing well in between the sections with your fingers.

13.   Remove the book from the press, and turn the boards over spine to foredge so that the glued edge is no longer in contact with the book. While the spine is still damp, knock the book level to the head and spine once more, to sort out any errant sections.

14.   Leave the glue for about 10 minutes, or until it is just dry to the touch. The book is now ready for rounding.

(i)   Lie the book on your bench with the foredge towards you.

(ii)   With the thumb of your left hand in the foredge and the rest of your hand on top of the book, gently hammer the sections towards you along the spine. Keep the backs of the section parallel and use your left hand to control the book, pulling with your fingers and pushing with your thumb.

(iii)   Turn the book over and repeat. Continue until an even curve appears.

The importance of swell will become apparent at this stage: insufficient swell will make the book difficult to round; too much swell will make the book over-round; uneven swell will produce correspondingly uneven round; with the correct amount of swell the round of the book should be an even curve. Very thin books will not require rounding.

15.   Mark up the depth of your joint. Set

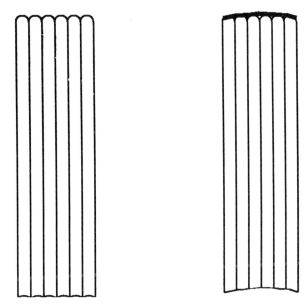

Fig 88   Too little swell.

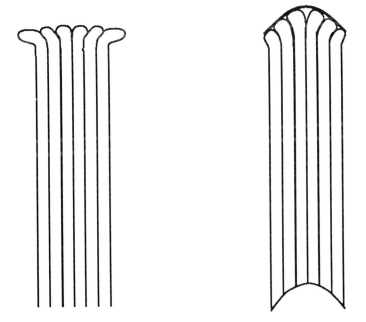

Fig 89   Too much swell.

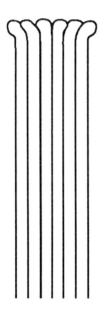 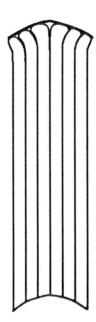

Fig 90   The correct amount of swell.

your dividers to the thickness of your board and, with one point on the endpaper fold, mark this distance on the waste sheet of your book at the head, middle and tail, front and back. Rule a fine pencil line along it.

16.   Place the book between backing boards and put it in the lying press. The wedge-shaped backing boards should be longer than the book. Check that the rounding of your book is symmetrical and that there are no slipped sections. Open the lying press so that the space between the cheeks is slightly less than the width of your book plus pressing boards.

(i)   Lie the book on the bench or lying press with about 1in (2.5cm) of the spine overlapping the edge. This will make picking up the book easier when the backing board is in position.

(ii)   Place the angled edge of the backing board on the pencilled line – the book should be positioned centrally with the tapes outside the board. Turn the book and pressing board over and place the second board in position.

(iii)   Holding the book and pressing boards firmly in the middle with your left hand, using your right hand to adjust the screws of the lying press, carefully lower the book between the cheeks so that it will lie mid-way between them. As the press accepts the book, adjust the screws, and gradually push the book and boards between the cheeks until the outer edges of the backing boards are level with the cheeks of the press. Both boards must be absolutely parallel and still in their original positions on the book. If they have moved, you must take the book out and start again.

(iv)   Using the press bar to ensure maximum pressure, tighten each screw of the press a little at a time, and finally check with dividers that the distance between each screw is identical.

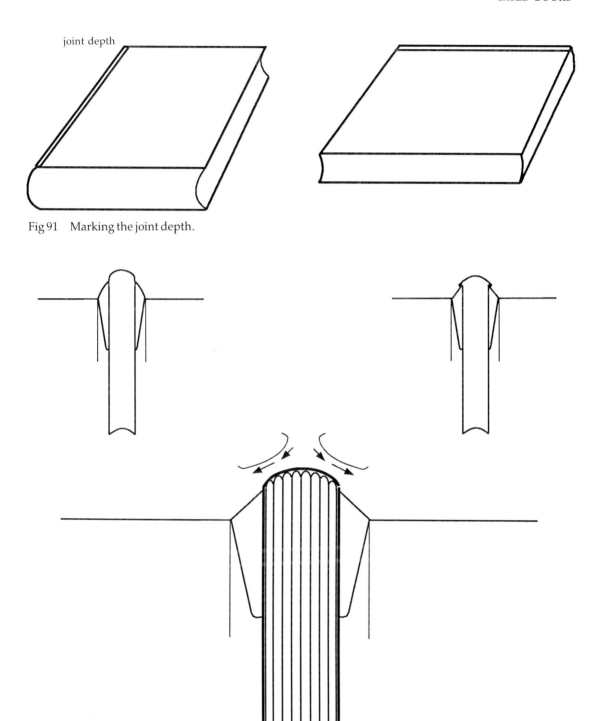

Fig 91   Marking the joint depth.

Fig 92   The backing boards in position.

(v)   Before you begin to back, check that the book is straight in the press by placing your L-square against the side of the press. The metal edge will pass over the pressing boards, and any inaccuracy of position will be clearly visible. If your L-square is not long enough, a spirit level will do.

(vi)   If you have too much swell in your spine, over-rounding will result. If you have ignored this until now you will be experiencing difficulty in tightening the press and keeping the book in place. When the press is tightened the centre sections will be forced up and the book will be distorted (it is rather like trying to clutch hold of a piece of wet soap). To remedy this, remove the book from the press and place sheets of heavy paper regularly throughout the book, parallel to and up to the joint line. They should be longer than the book and greater in depth than the depth of the pressing board to avoid marking the paper. The number required will depend upon the book.

17.   Back the book. When a book is backed, the sections are hammered over each other until the endpapers lie on the angled edge of the backing boards. When

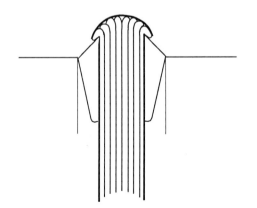

Fig 93   Backing.

the book is taken out of the press the paper will relax and the joint will form a right angle.

Standing at one end of the press, and using the rounded face of the hammer, gently but firmly with glancing blows start to hammer over the sections. Observe the following rules:

● Start from the head and work down the sections to the tail.
● Although the very centre sections are left unhammered, work from the middle and gradually work your way right and left to the outside.
● Concentrate on hammering one or two sections at a time. Avoid the temptation to 'cheat' and hammer over the outer sections. The sections must be worked on methodically so that each overlaps the next.
● Remember that swinging hammer blows will damage the book and the press. Your hammer blows should be firm and concentrated on the sections on which you are working. It can help if the hammer is held fairly close to the head as this affords a greater degree of control.

When you are satisfied that your backing is complete, spend a few minutes working on the outer sections, making sure they are firmly down on the backing boards. Smooth the spine down with a bone folder.

18.   Remove the book from the press, placing one hand underneath to prevent it falling out as the screws are untightened.

19.   Now that the book has been rounded and backed, protect your newly-formed joint by keeping the book safely between its rough boards, with the boards up to but not over the joint.

20. Trim the endpapers to fit the book. It is a sad fact that absolutely square books are rare. However, the boards and endpapers of your book *must* be square. Take your dividers and place one point exactly in the joint at the head. Lift the endpapers and adjust the dividers so that the second point is on the foredge of the book. Repeat at the middle and tail, thus finding the widest point, and then repeat at the back of the book. When you have established the maximum width of the book from joint to foredge, lie the book on the bench and, with one point of the dividers in the joint, carefully mark this maximum width at head and tail of your endpapers. Place a thin cutting board beneath the endpapers and trim with a knife and a straight edge. Trim the tail. If there is any discrepancy in page length trim to the longest page.

21. Line the spine.
(i) Place the book in the lying press, between rough boards, with 1in (2.5cm) protruding.
(ii) Glue the spine.
(iii) Mull – remember that the mull should cover the kettle stitches and overlap the spine by 1in (2.5cm) on each side.
(iv) Glue and line with Kraft paper, rubbing the paper down well with your bone folder. A second lining of Kraft paper will be needed for larger books.

22. Remove the book from the press and cut the boards to size. The square should be the same as the board thickness, and the length of the boards is therefore the length of the book plus two thicknesses of

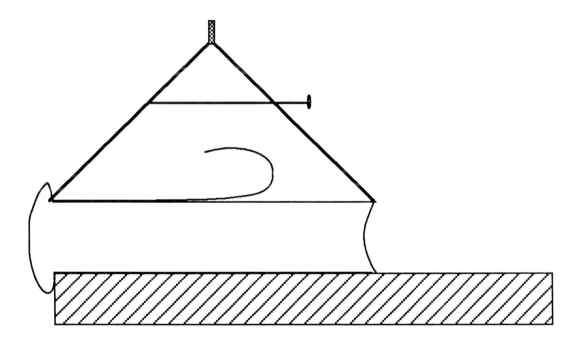

Fig 94   Measuring the widest part of the book preparatory to trimming the endpapers.

board. As in flat-back binding, the board is moved forward from the joint by one board thickness. Therefore, if the board is cut to the exact width of the book from joint to foredge when it is eventually placed in its true position, the square on the foredge will be correct.

23. Cut a manila spine piece the length of the boards by the width of the rounded spine. Measure the spine width by wrapping a strip of paper around it from edge to edge, and measuring the result with dividers.

24. Cut out the cloth and make the case using the same methods as described on pages 75–76. The only difference is the joint

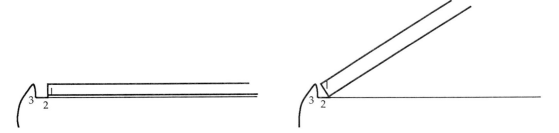

Fig 95   Joint allowance.

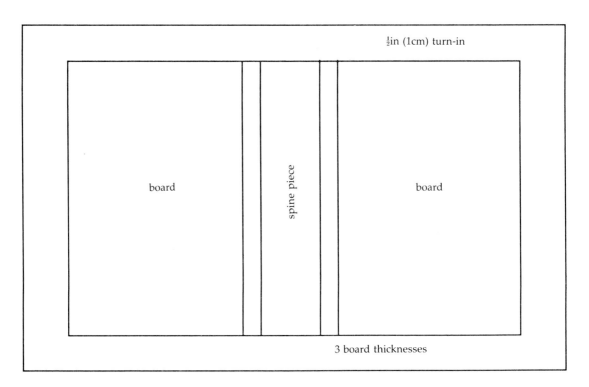

Fig 96   Marking out the cloth.

allowance which should be three board thicknesses.

25.   Glue the cloth, make the case, and allow to dry.

26.   Case the book.

(i)   Before you start, discreetly mark the squares at the head, tail and foredge on the inside of the case.

(ii)   Work the inside of the spine piece of the case against the edge of your bench to curve it slightly.

(iii)   Tear out the waste sheet of your endpapers by placing a metal ruler to the fold and tearing the outer page cleanly away.

(iv)   Placing waste paper beneath the coloured board paper, case the book in as described on page 76 of flat-back binding. As your work speed increases, you should be able to paste down both endpapers and then nip. Remove the book from the press, and work the cloth into the French groove with your bone folder through a piece of waste paper.

27.   Dry.

Summary

1.   Collate.
2.   Make endpapers.
3.   Cut boards.
4.   Pull.
5.   Knock out old joint.
6.   Guard.
7.   Mark up for sewing.
8.   Sew.
9.   Knock out excess swell.
10.   Glue up spine (plough foredge).
11.   Paste up first two and last two sections.
12.   Round.
13.   Back (plough head and tail).
14.   Trim endpapers.
15.   Line the spine.
16.   Cut boards and spine piece to size.
17.   Mark out and cut the cloth.
18.   Make the case.
19.   Letter.
20.   Case the book.

8 Ploughing

Most of the books you re-case or repair will not need trimming, but it is useful to know how to plough, particularly if you make up blank books of your own. It is possible to trim books with a guillotine, and this is not to be confused with a board cutter. Guillotines can be either large electrical machines or smaller manual creatures, and consist basically of a metal bed, a moveable back gauge, a clamp and a blade which descends and cuts from left to right. It is certainly not necessary for the amateur binder to own one as their uses are mainly commercial and the cut and finish given by a plough blade is infinitely superior.

Fig 97   Small electric guillotine.

PLOUGHING THE HEAD AND TAIL OF A CASED BOOK

The forwarding of the book is as described for a cased binding except where mentioned.

1. Collate.
2. Make endpapers.
3. Cut boards. The rough boards must be thicker than the actual boards – if necessary glue two boards together.
4. Pull.
5. Knock out old joint.
6. Guard and repair.
7. Mark up for sewing. You are going to trim a small amount off the head, and this must be accounted for now. Trim off the minimum amount of paper – if you cut off too much you will spoil the imposition of the type on the page. If the head is uneven, trim just below the shortest page, otherwise $\frac{1}{16}$ to $\frac{1}{8}$in depending upon the size of the book should be adequate. Mark the amount to be trimmed on the spine, and measure from this point instead of the head when marking up for sewing. If the tail is to be trimmed the same rules apply. Remove the endpapers and saw the cerf.
8. Sew.
9. Knock out the excess swell.
10. Glue up the spine.
11. Paste up the first two and last two sections.
12. Round.
13. Back.
14. Plough.
(i) Having removed the book from the press, turn the press over on to the ploughing side.
(ii) The joint of your book will be its one known absolutely straight line. You will have already decided and marked on your spine how much you are going to plough from the head. Placing a set square along the joint, mark the trimming line along the head of the front waste sheet using a very sharp hard pencil.
(iii) Place the book between the thick rough boards – the extra thickness of the boards ensures that the joints of the book are protected. Make sure that the boards are absolutely square. The back board is placed up to the joint and protrudes $\frac{1}{4}$in (5mm) from the head, the front board up to the joint and on the cutting line.
(iv) Place the book in the lying press, as always making sure that it is in the middle of the press. The runners should be on your left-hand side and the spine of the book towards you when you are standing at the end of the press. Gradually lower the book into the press until the cutting line and board is exactly level with the cheek of the press. Check that the book is straight in the press and that it has not twisted – the trimming line across the spine will help you with this. If the book has shifted, take it out and start again. When you are satisfied with the position of the book, do up the screws as tightly as possible; check that the distance between the cheeks is identical, and then you are ready to plough.
(v) Your plough blade should lie absolutely flat on both cheeks of your press. If it does not, a little packing with paper between the blade and its metal holder may be necessary.
(vi) Standing at the end of the press, with the plough runners on your left, place the left-hand cheek of the plough between the runners. By turning the handle, open the plough so that the cheeks are slightly wider apart than the width of the book.
(vii) With both cheeks of the plough on

Fig 98   Plough in position on lying press.

those of the press, run the plough down the press past the book. Lift the right-hand cheek of the plough, and run it back towards you, keeping the left-hand cheek in the runners. On the second return journey, turn the handle by a fraction, thus moving the blade closer to the book. Once the blade has made contact with the paper, continue with this rhythmical movement, cutting only away from you, and moving the blade a fraction at a time. If you try to cut too many pages at once the paper could tear. The aim is to cut one or two pages at a time.

(viii)   When the head is ploughed, cut off the remaining trimmings on the back joint with a sharp knife held flat to the head of the book, and carefully remove the book

from the press. The paper off-cuts should have completely smooth cut edges.If they are crinkled or rough you are either trying to cut too many pages at once, the book is not held tightly enough in the press, or your plough blade is blunt.

If the tail of the book is to be ploughed it is done in exactly the same way. Usually the tail is only trimmed if the foredge is also ploughed.

15.   Trim endpapers.
16.   Line spine.
17.   Cut boards and spine piece.
18.   Make case.
19.   Letter.
20.   Case in.

Heads and tails are always ploughed after rounding and backing as the amount of swell present before would make it impossible to hold the book accurately in the press. (Please note that ploughing 'in boards' applies only to leather-bound books.)

FOREDGES

If it is necessary to plough the foredge of a cased book (for example, if you have made the book yourself), then the ploughing has to be done *before* the book is rounded and backed. The slight drawback to this is that, when the book is finally rounded and backed, although the foredge will be improved, instead of a smooth curve it will be slightly stepped, particularly if the sections are thick (Fig 99). Proceed as for cased binding, but, after glueing up the spine and before rounding and backing, plough the foredge. To combat the swell in the spine, a pair of thick boards with chamfered edges are necessary. The chamfer or bevel should be at least 1in (2.5cm) long (Fig 100(b)). Proceed as follows:

Fig 99   Stepped foredge.

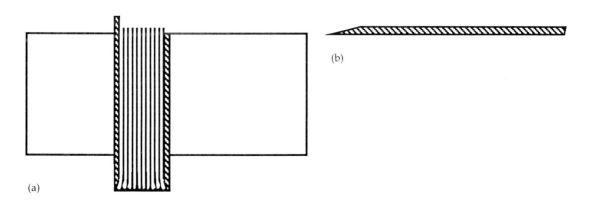

(a)

(b)

Fig 100   (a) The book in the press ready for ploughing between chamfered boards (b).

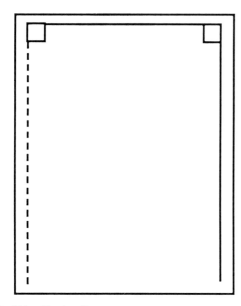

Fig 101   Cutting lines.

1.   Mark the joint depth from your spine edge as usual.

2.   From this, mark your cutting edge along the head – this will give you a right angle from which to drop the trimming line on the foredge (Fig 101).

3.   Take one of your thick chamfered boards and cut it so that in width it measures from the spine edge of the book to the cutting line.

4.   Place the book between the boards, knocking it absolutely flat on the spine. The bevels of the board should be on the inside so that they accommodate the swell of the spine. The back board should project by $\frac{1}{2}$in (1cm) and the front board should be just to the cutting line.

5.   Position the book in the ploughing side of the press and proceed as before.

(Please note that only cased books have their foredges ploughed in this way.)

9 Library-Style Binding

Library-style binding was developed as a strong yet economical way of binding reference books. Traditionally it is a half-leather binding, but it can also be made successfully using buckram or book-cloth.

1. Prepare the work surface.
2. Make the endpapers.

(i) For each end, cut two folded whites and two single coloureds, $\frac{1}{2}$in (1cm) longer and $\frac{1}{2}$in (1cm) wider than your book when folded. Cut a strip of cloth for each end to match your covering cloth – the length of your endpapers, by $\frac{3}{4}$ to $1\frac{1}{4}$in (15–30mm) wide, according to the size of your book. As always, the grain of cloth and paper should run from head to tail, and the weights of the paper should be as similar as possible.

(ii) Halve your cloth strips vertically, and on the reverse side mark the mid-points.

(iii) Glue the reverse side of the cloth and place the two folded whites on to it, edge to edge, along the mid-point line, allowing a gap of $\frac{1}{16}$in (1.25mm) between them. Rub the cloth down firmly.

(iv) With the cloth strip facing you, paste one outer white, protecting the cloth strip with a sheet of waste and placing waste paper underneath it as usual. On to it place one single colour so that it just overlaps the cloth. Repeat with the second colour on to the other facing white. Nip, with clean waste protecting all papers.

(v) Allow to dry, by hanging up for a short time, and then placing under a light weight. Remember to replace the waste sheets regularly.

(vi) Repeat with the second endpaper.

(vii) When the endpapers are dry, trim off the excess colour on the foredge and

Hand tools	Equipment	Materials
Pencil	Pressing boards	Waste paper
Bone folder	Nipping press	Kraft paper
Scissors	Backing boards	Tape
Dividers	Weight	Manila
Needle	Lying press	Cloth
Scalpel	Knocking down iron	Guarding paper
Straight edge		Mull
Glue and paste brushes		Thread
		Glue and paste
		Paper for endpapers – two sheets of white, one sheet of coloured
		Board, thick and thin
		Thread, coloured to match the cloth

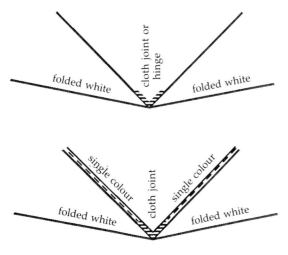

Fig 102   Library-style endpapers.

fold the endpapers with the colours in-side.

3.   Cut two thick and two thin boards, ½in (1cm) longer and ½in (1cm) wider than the book – ⅛in (2.5mm) and 1/16in (1.25mm) board is a good combination for most books. Taking the thinner board, glue all but a 1in (2.5cm) strip along one of the long edges – this is best accomplished by measuring 1in (2.5cm) along the board, masking it off with a piece of waste paper folded across the grain. Holding the waste in position, glue away from it. Wipe excess glue from the edges of the board and place the thicker board on top, knocking level to the unglued edge. Nip and allow to dry overnight.

4.   Collate book.

5.   Pull.

6.   Mark up for sewing.

7.   Remove endpapers and saw cerf.

8.   Sew – for heavier books the following method of sewing is useful.

(i)   Prick the sewing holes through the centre of the cloth joint on your endpap-ers.

(ii)   Using coloured silk thread, or nor-mal sewing thread dyed to match your cloth strip, sew your first endpaper.

(iii)   Change to normal sewing thread. Take the first section and insert the needle at the kettle stitch as usual, leaving a tail of 2in (5cm) to tie to the endpaper thread. Instead of simply coming out of the sec-tion, around the tape and in again, come out of the section, and catch up the stitch immediately below with your needle be-fore going back into the section. This link-ing stitch is continued throughout, and the kettle stitches are formed as normal. Do not pull the thread too tightly as this could result in the sections being pulled back, with (in extreme cases) a convex foredge. This method of sewing can also be used on just the first three and last three sections for added strength on other books. (Fig 103.)

9.   Knock out excess swell.

10.   Glue up the spine between the tapes.

11.   Paste up first two and last two sec-tions.

12.   Round.

13.   Back.

14.   Trim endpapers using dividers.

15.   Glue and line the spine with mull, allowing 1in (2.5cm) to overlap on each side.

16.   Cut the boards to size: the length should equal the length of the book plus two board thicknesses; the width equals the width of the book from joint to for-edge.

17.   Attach the boards.

(i)   Mark the square of the book on the inside of the boards – the thinner board goes to the inside, next to the book. Also mark the width of the groove from your joint (one board thickness) to give another guide or pitching line for attaching the boards accurately.

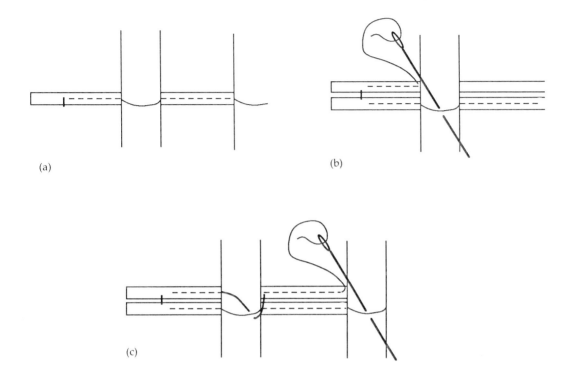

Fig 103   (a), (b) and (c) Sewing.

(ii)   Make the flange to be inserted into the split in the boards.

Place a sheet of waste paper beneath the outer sheet of the endpaper at the front of your book.

Glue the paper, including under the tapes and mull. Before allowing them to stick to the paper, run your bone folder along the joint over the mull and tapes, so that they follow the contours of the book.

Fold the glued sheet in half so that the mull and tapes are sandwiched. Rub down firmly.

Trim the flange to 1in (2.5cm) and mitre the corners, then repeat at the back.

(iii)   Open the split in your boards with a bone folder and glue the space with a narrow brush.

(iv)   Insert the front flange into the glued split of the front board and adjust until the squares are equal. The easiest way is to slide the board along the flange. Repeat with the back board.

(v)   Nip the book. Place tin plates inside and outside the boards, with the edges to the spine edge of the boards, and the pressing boards also to the edge of the boards at the spine. Remove from the press and allow to dry under a weight.

18.   Line the spine with Kraft paper. When a library-style binding is bound in leather, the leather is pasted directly on to the lined spine – the leather remains flexible, and the opening of the book is therefore not impaired. However, buckram and book cloth are not as flexible and cannot be stuck directly to the spine, so a hollow tube must be made to separate the cloth from the spine.

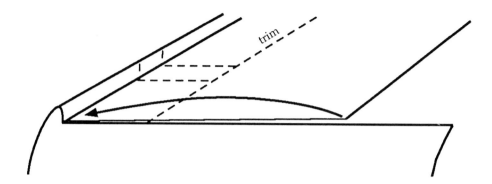

Fig 104 Folding the glued waste sheet around the mull and tapes.

(i) Place the book in the lying press for glueing. Although it now has its boards attached, rough boards should still be used as protection.

(ii) Take a piece of Kraft paper $3\frac{1}{2}$ to 4 times the width of the spine, and about 1in (2.5cm) longer.

(iii) Find the width of your spine and mark this measurement along from one long straight edge of your Kraft paper. Fold along this line.

(iv) Glue the spine of your book. If it is a heavy book, it is a good idea to give it a preliminary lining of Kraft paper to provide extra strength. If the sewing and tapes are particularly prominent, give as smooth a hollow as possible by lining the spine between the tapes, cutting the Kraft to fit the spaces exactly.

(v) If necessary, reglue the spine. Position your folded Kraft paper so that the folded edge lies exactly along the opposite spine edge from you. Rub down firmly.

(vi) The middle of your Kraft is now glued to the spine. Bring the measured

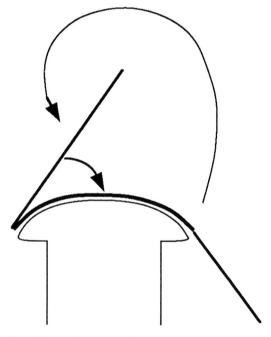

Fig 105 Making the hollow.

flap over and, holding it firmly in place, glue the outer side. Bring over the second flap and rub it down firmly on top of the glued surface. Fold back any excess Kraft along the long spine edge and trim off. You should now have a hollow tube consisting of one layer of paper glued to the spine, and two glued together. This is called a 'one on and two off hollow'.

I have found that adding a thin manila spine piece, curved by rubbing it against the edge of a bench and glued to the outer part of the hollow, or an extra layer of Kraft paper, is a help when covering, as the two thicknesses of Kraft can crumple when the cloth is turned in.

18. Trim the hollow so that it is level with the height of the boards.
19. Make a slit of $\frac{3}{4}$in (15mm) in the hollow on each side, head and tail. Also slit the flange where it is exposed between the boards and the spine to the same depth, to allow for the passage of the cloth turn-in.
20. Trim the inside of the hollow – the Kraft that is glued to the spine only – so that it is flush with the head and tail of the book.
21. Cap the book. To protect the pages and to prevent the book from falling open and hindering the covering processes, a piece of brown paper is wrapped around the pages of the book, completely enclosing them.
(i) Cut a piece of paper $2\frac{1}{2}$ times the length of the book by the width of the book plus one thickness of the book plus $1\frac{1}{2}$in (3.5cm).
(ii) With the capping paper inside the boards, wrap it around the text and endpapers lengthwise, holding it in place with sticky tape. Slit the overlapping paper at the corners at the head and tail and

turn in the flaps on the foredge. To avoid a mass of paper on the foredge, trim off the top sheet level with the foredge, before turning over the paper head and tail, and bringing up the foredge flap to envelop the book.
22. Cut out and mark the cloth for covering.
(i) Mark a turn-in of $\frac{5}{8}$ to 1in (12.5–25mm), according to the size of the book and the thickness of the boards.
(ii) Lie the book on the cloth with the head of the board on the turn-in, and draw around the board, marking the spine edge.
(iii) Measure and mark the joint allowance of three board thicknesses.
(iv) Mark the spine width, measuring the rounded spine with a strip of paper first.
(v) Mark the second joint, draw around the second board, and then mark the turn-in on the remaining three sides.
23. Glue the cloth.
(i) Lie the book flat on the cloth, head and foredge to markers. Turn over and rub down, moving the book to the edge of the bench so that the rest of the cloth hangs down out of the way.
(ii) Holding the board in position, work the cloth along the groove with a bone folder through the paper.
(iii) Wrap the cloth around the spine and rub down well.
(iv) Turn the book over and work the cloth into the second groove and on to the second board.
(v) Mitre the corners.
(vi) Stand the book on its tail – if the book is heavy, support the text with a piece of board. Turn in the cloth at the head, starting with the spine. Open the boards to open the hollow, thus facilitating the turning in of the cloth, and

Fig 106   Half-cloth library-style binding.

Fig 107 Inside board of a library-style binding.

allowing it to pass through the slits made for it in the hollow and the flanges to the inside of the board. Having turned in the cloth at the spine, work along the board edges, making sure that the cloth is well stuck. Sharpen the turn-in at the spine by lying the book flat on its spine, and working along it with your bone folder. Repeat at the tail. Turn in the sides and corners.

24. Work along the French groove again with bone folder through waste paper.

25. Leave to dry with waste papers inside.

26. The French groove can be further improved by inserting knitting needles – the size will depend upon the thickness of the groove, but they must be longer than the book – into the groove. Put tin plates inside the boards and outside so that the needles are covered, and then place between pressing boards and nip. If the needles are held together at the head and tail with elastic bands, the possibility of them moving and damaging the book is lessened.

27. If there is any discrepancy in the turn-in widths, trim to the narrowest measurement.

28. Trim the board papers so that they overlap the cloth turn-ins by $\frac{1}{32}$in (0.6mm). Library endpapers are put down with the board closed and you trim the board paper by marking with the board more or less closed on to the book – this is particularly important at the foredge. As an experiment, hold the foredge of the board paper with the board nearly closed, and then open the board. You will feel the endpaper move inwards, demonstrating the difference between measuring the endpaper with the board open and with the board closed.

(i) Set your dividers to the required width.

(ii) Holding the endpaper firmly with the board closed, lift the board and endpaper just enough to allow you to mark the required trimming width from the inside edge of the board on to the endpaper at the foredge head and tail. Two, or at most three, divider marks should suffice along each edge – any more will be confusing.

(iii) With a piece of thin card beneath the board paper, trim with a scalpel and straight edge. At the head and tail stop about $\frac{3}{4}$in (15mm) away from the cloth strip (again your distance will depend upon the size of the book) and finish by mitreing the paper to the cloth.

29. Paste down the endpapers.

(i) Paste the board paper with waste paper beneath it to protect the book.

(ii) Remove the waste, having wiped around the edges of the pasted endpaper to remove excess paste, and close the board on to the book.

(iii) Repeat with the other endpaper.

(iv) Nip.

30. Dry, leaving the book under a light weight with dry waste sheets inside and out and pressing boards up to the joint. Change the waste sheets regularly.

Summary

1. Collate.
2. Make endpapers.
3. Cut and prepare split boards.
4. Pull.
5. Knock out old joints.
6. Guard and repair.
7. Mark up for sewing.
8. Sew.
9. Knock out swell.
10. Glue up spine.
11. Paste up first two sections and last two sections.

12. Round.
13. Back.
14. Trim endpapers.
15. Glue and line spine with mull.
16. Make the flange.
17. Cut boards to size.
18. Attach boards, nip and allow to dry.
19. Glue up spine, line with Kraft paper and make hollow.
20. Cut out the cloth.
21. Cover – you may find it easier to glue the boards of the book rather than the cloth to begin with.
22. Finish.
23. Trim out inside boards.
24. Trim board papers.
25. Put down endpapers, nip and allow to dry.

10 Finishing

One of the most rewarding aspects of bookbinding is finishing – that is, the lettering and decorating of the book. Good lettering should be unremarkable. The reader should be able to read the title and author easily, and if he notices the spacing of the letters and wonders whether they are too close together or too far apart, then there is something wrong.

Before you begin tooling on your book it is essential to practise. Although cloth cases can be lettered flat it is also useful to learn to letter on a rounded spine. A false book spine can easily be made from wood, which can be covered with cloth or leather as required.

Hand tools	Equipment	Materials
Pencil	Finishing stove	Foil
Ruler	Hand letters	Board
Dividers	Lying or finishing press	Manila, or vellum strip
		Masking tape
		Detail paper (available from art shops in pads)
		Cotton wool in a saucer

HOW TO START

1. Tape a piece of detail paper to a piece of board; the paper must be held firmly.
2. Put your letters on the finishing stove, with the handles in the indented ring and just the face of each tool on the heating surface. Even if you are only practising on paper, it is a good idea to put the tools out like this – not only will you know where each letter is, but there will also be no danger of them rolling off the bench and damaging themselves.
3. Rule a line on your piece of paper. Take your first letter. Try to get into the habit of glancing at the face of the letter as you take it from the stove – this will not only ensure that you have picked up the correct one, but also that it is the right way up. To help with this last problem there is a small line on the shaft of each letter marking the head.
4. Holding the wooden handle of your letter firmly in your right hand, and using the tip of your left thumbnail as a guide, carefully lower the letter on to the paper so that the head of the letter just touches the line and the rest hangs from it at right angles to the line (*see* below).

Fig 108   Finishing stove with tools.

5.   Once the letter is down, rock it from head to tail and side to side, so you are virtually following the shape of the letter. Lift the letter from the paper and inspect the impression. You should be looking for the following points:

- Straightness
- Evenness of pressure
- A firm, but not too deep, impression

Each letter is slightly different to put down. You will probably find that the 'square' letters, such as M and N, and the round letters (O, C, and so on) are easier to put down than, say, As, Ls and Js, but with practice you will eventually get them all right.

SECOND STEP

When you are used to handling the letters, try writing different words, concentrating on the straightness and the spacing of the letters. The spacing of letters is best judged by the eye, but as a starting point the following may be a useful exercise:

1.   Write out the title or word to be lettered.
2.   Set out the letters in order of use on the finishing stove. Keep this order so that you know exactly where each letter is, no matter how many times it has to be put down.
3.   Set your dividers to the width of the widest letter of the alphabet (M or W).

111

4. Rule a line on your detail paper and walk your dividers along the line, making an equally-spaced mark for each letter. If you have more than one word on a line allow one letter space between each word. Similarly, when spacing out lines of lettering, the distance between each line is usually the height of one letter. As before, hang the letters from the line, the marks being central (Fig 109(a)).

5. Look carefully at each word and adjust the letters as necessary. The Os in Fig 109(b) need perhaps a little more space, whereas the Is need a little less around them (Fig 109(c)). Re-letter until the spacing looks correct. With practice you should be able to get most words correctly

spaced by eye at the first attempt. Try imagining that you are filling the gaps between the letters with sand – you should need the same amount of sand for each space. (Fig 110.)

LETTERING ON FOIL

1. Prepare the finishing stove, letters, cotton wool in a saucer, a jug of cold water, a stiff brush, cloth securely taped to a piece of board, foil, crocus paper and a scrap of leather for polishing the toll faces.

2. Put a 'sausage' of cotton wool in a saucer of cold water – the cotton wool should be thoroughly wet and still sit in a pool of water. Use this to cool the tools as

(a)

(b)
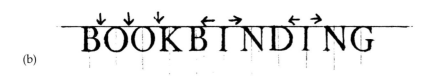

(c)

Fig 109(a), (b) and (c)   Experimenting with spacing and adjusting it accordingly.

BOOKBINDING

Fig 110   The correct spacing for the word 'Bookbinding'.

112

they come off the stove. Never allow the face of the tool to become wet, as drops of water can lodge in the little crevices of the face with disastrous effects on the tooling. Lay the shank of the tool on the cotton wool and turn it around to cool it. Do not allow your wet cotton wool to heat up as this will affect the temperature of your tool – keep turning it in its pool of water, adding or replacing the cold water as necessary.

3. Find out the correct temperature for cooling.

(i) Set out your tools on the finishing stove and switch it on. Most foils have a recommended working temperature and most modern stoves have a temperature gauge, so set your dial to the appropriate temperature.

(ii) Secure a piece of foil to your cloth-covered board with masking tape.

(iii) Take one heated letter. Cool it until it has stopped sizzling entirely – this is known as 'off the sizzle'.

(iv) Briefly polish the face of the tool by rubbing it on the reverse side of your scrap of leather. If your tools are new, it is a good idea to rub them on a piece of crocus paper (something known as 'rouge paper') before beginning.

4. Tool an impression, rocking the tool head to tail and side to side as before, and dwelling in the impression for perhaps one or two seconds before lifting the tool off. Count five seconds and repeat, five seconds and repeat, until you have a row of letters.

5. Lift the foil and inspect your work. You are aiming for a bright, solid, clean impression, and this is obtained by using the correct temperature, the right amount of dwell, and the correct pressure. A fuzzy-edged impression means that the tool was either too hot or your dwell was too long. A faint impression results either if the tool is too cold, or if insufficient dwell or pressure is allowed.

Smaller tools generally need less pressure and dwell than larger ones. Select the best impression and note how it was made – how cool the tool was, the polish given, the weight, the number of seconds, and the amount of dwell. If you accustom yourself to working to a rhythm, and avoid all temptation to hurry, you will find these preliminary exercises worth-while.

LETTERING THE CASE

As cased bindings are lettered *before* the book is cased in, it is possible to letter the case flat. This is reasonably straightfor-ward.

LETTERING THE SPINE

Spines can be lettered either across, up or down. When deciding, as always consid-er the age and style of the book. The most traditional way is to letter *across* the spine, but if this is not possible because the book is too thin, then it must be lettered down or up. The more traditional way is *up* the spine, although many 'coffee-table' and modern books are lettered down.

Lettering Up or Down the Spine

1. Prepare the finishing bench and set out your tools.

2. Write out the title and author clearly, checking that the spelling is correct. It is usual to use as brief a form of the title as

possible. Thus the 'Poetical Works of Alexander Pope Esq. with a Sketch of the Author's Life' could be reduced to 'Pope's Works' or 'Poems of Pope'.

3. Work out the title as before on a piece of detail paper taped to board. Allow one letter space (M) between each word of the title, and more to separate the author and title – this distance will depend on the length of the spine, but it *must* be clear that the author's name is not a part of the title. Usually only the surname is used, but if initials are to be included, leave one letter space between them.

4. When your title is satisfactory (and you will often need more than one attempt), prepare your case for finishing by lying the case flat on the bench. Cut a piece of board longer than the length of the book boards by the width of the spine piece plus the two joint allowances. Insert this strip between the boards to provide a firm base for tooling – this is not necessary for flat-backed books.

5. Tape a strip of foil firmly in position along the spine.

6. When working out where your foil should go, remember that the optical centre is always higher than the true centre. For this reason there should be more space allowed at the tail than at the head. To work out where the line of letters must go, so that they travel up or down the exact middle of the spine width:

(i) Measure the width of your spine.

(ii) Mark the width on your detail paper and board. Subtract from this width the height of one letter.

(iii) Halve the remaining measurement which, when measured from the spine edge, will give you the correct point from which your letters should be hung. Mark this line on the foil using dividers and a

straight edge – do this carefully as it is possible to mark the cloth.

7. Cut out the blind plan of your title. The cut beneath the letters is the most crucial, and should be as close to the letters as possible without actually touching them.

8. Tape the blind plan in position on the spine of your book, just above your guide line. Mark the centres of the letters by making little tick marks along the foil guide line. As you become more proficient you will be able to dispense with these and tool directly from your guide.

9. Take up your first letter. Check it is the right way up, cool it and polish it. Position the letter above the foil, pause and tool.

If you have difficulty in putting any letter down straight, have a few practices on a piece of detail paper and board first, so that you get the feel of the letter before re-heating and tooling it.

10. Remove the foil. With your brush remove any excess foil from the cloth and inspect the lettering. If any letters have not taken properly, cut a small piece of foil, take the offending letter off the stove, and cool and polish it as before. Place the letter in the impression, and rock it, lifting its head but keeping its tail in position. Slip the piece of foil underneath and re-tool. Repeat with the tail if necessary.

Lettering Across the Spine

Proceed as for lettering up or down the spine. The only difference will be in setting out the title. Work out carefully how you are going to position your words, bearing in mind the ultimate shape, and the fact that the title must be read easily and be instantly understandable. It must also fit comfortably across the width of the spine – nothing looks worse than letters falling over the edge. If necessary break the word and hyphenate it. Having decided on how your title is to be lettered, prepare the blind pattern as before, working out the separate lines accurately.

1. Lay the case flat on the bench, with a supporting piece of board under the spine piece (as before) if the book is cased.
2. Tape the foil in position.
3. Using dividers, measure the width of the spine, halve this and mark the vertical centre line down the foil.
4. To work out where your title is to go, divide the spine into six imaginary panels. As the optical centre is always slightly higher than the true centre, when

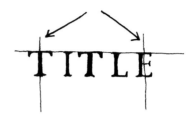

Fig 112   Finding the middle of a word.

measuring panels (even imaginary ones) the tail panel is slightly longer than the head panel, which in turn is slightly longer than the remaining panels. To achieve this, measure from a point $\frac{1}{2}$in (1cm) above the tail to a point $\frac{1}{4}$in (5mm) below the head (or from the tail kettle stitch to halfway between the head kettle stitch and the head), and divide that portion of the spine by six. Your title will be positioned where the second panel would be.
5. With the point of your dividers and a straight edge, mark the first line of your tooling across the foil, measuring from the head. Cut out the appropriate part of your pattern, having first marked the mid-point of the words by halving the distance from the middle of the first letter to the middle of the last.
6. Position the blind pattern just above your tooling line as before, holding it in place with masking tape, and tool.
7. Repeat for the second and following lines, allowing one letter height between the lines. The space between the author's name and the title is at least two letter heights.

Lettering on a Curved Spine

Library-style books have to be lettered on to the curved spine, and it is also possible to letter cased books in this way, positioning the book in the case before the

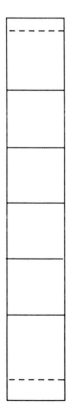

Fig 111   Positioning the title.

Fig 113   The face of the tool at right angles to the spine of the book.

endpapers are put down. Place the book between rough boards in a lying or finishing press, making sure that the spine is angled so that you can tool it comfortably. You should be able to position the tool so that the face touches the foil at right angles to the book.

When ruling the lines across the spine, use either a strip of paper (folded across the grain) or a straight-edged strip of vellum or perspex as a guide. Note also that, as you are tooling on a curved surface, you will have to move to ensure that the tool, particularly on the outer curves of the spine, always touches the book at right angles to it.

Fig 114   Book held in small finishing press.

116

LETTERING THE FRONT BOARD

The front board of a book is not always lettered, but it would be necessary in the case of, for example, a visitors' book. Again, the lettering must be slightly higher than the true centre. When finding the mid-point of the width of the book, remember to include the rounded spine or the spine piece in the measurement. Measure from a to b (Fig 115), not merely from board edge to board edge, cut out a piece of paper the same size and shape as your title and place it in position on the book. Remember that, although no one is going to check your measurements with a ruler, they will notice if the title is not straight or just does not look right. Before tooling, place a tin plate beneath the board to give as hard a working surface as possible and to protect the book.

An alternative method of tooling with foil is to tool through the blind paper impression on to the foil beneath. Care must be taken to ensure that the paper is very firmly secured as the two surfaces

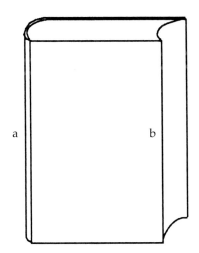

Fig 115   Finding the mid-point of the front cover.

will tend to slide. You will also have to practise tooling through the paper on to foil to find the correct tooling temperature – this will be slightly hotter than when tooling directly on to foil. This method is particularly useful for tooling small designs on to foil.

DECORATIVE TOOLING

Although most cloth bindings are fairly simple and therefore need only the minimum amount of tooling, it is possible to make up and execute simple designs. Very intricately-patterned tools are not usually suitable as the weave of the cloth can interfere with the pattern.

PALLETS AND FILLETS

Lines across the spine are tooled with a special spine pallet (see pages 32–33). Although this is more often seen on leather bindings, decorative gold lines can be put on to a cloth spine.

(i)   Place the book in a lying or finishing press, with the spine parallel to the cheeks of the press, but protruding by about 2in (5cm).

(ii)   Tape the foil securely in position.

(iii)   With dividers measure from the head of the book and mark exactly where the line is to be, using a vellum strip as described before, either with a sharp bone folder or divider tip.

(iv)   Heat and cool the pallet. You will find that larger tools heat up quickly, so beware of over-heating – a very hot tool will make no sizzle at first on the cooler, and if your pallet has been on the stove for quite a time, you should be aware of this.

(v)   Starting from the spine edge nearest

to you, and standing squarely, firmly and carefully follow your guide line across the spine, keeping an equal pressure and dwell all the time. Repeat as desired.

Decorative gold lines or borders on the front board are made using a fillet (*see* pages 33–34) or decorative roll. Decorative rolls can be difficult to put down satisfactorily on cloth, so a plain line using a fillet is best, possibly in conjunction with a simple corner tool. You will also need a small $\frac{1}{4}$in (5mm) pallet the same width (or point size) as your fillet. As before, mark your line with dividers and then draw it on the foil with a sharp bone folder and straight edge. As it can be difficult to know exactly where to start or stop with a fillet, the corners or beginnings and ends of the lines are tooled first using the small pallet.

Starting from inside the pallet line, tool steadily along your marked line with your heated fillet. The straight side of the wheel is your sight line and should therefore be to the left.

It is not as easy as it sounds to tool a straight line with a fillet, so practise first by marking lines on design paper taped to board with a bone folder. When you can keep to these lines with your fillet, adv-

ance to tooling through foil on to cloth. Always make sure that you are comfortable when tooling, and that when using the fillet you can reach the whole length of the line without standing on tiptoe. If necessary make yourself a little platform from bricks or wood.

Gold or 'blind' (non-coloured) lines can also look effective when tooled along the cloth edges of half- or quarter-cloth bindings. A warm fillet tooled along the edge of the paper at the spine and corners finishes off these bindings, even if no gold is used. Mark your line first with a sharp bone folder before tooling.

DECORATIVE TOOLS

Simple decorative tooling can be accomplished by marking clearly on the foil where the tool has to go and tooling directly on to the foil. More complicated designs using gouges can be executed as follows:

1. Make a clear drawing of your intended design.
2. Trace the design on to detail paper using a hard sharp pencil.

Fig 116   Working out a simple design with different gouges.

Fig 117   Example of relief design on cloth-cased book (the work of one of the
author's students).

3. Tape a clean piece of detail paper to some board, and tape your traced design on top of this. The under impression will give you an idea of how the design will look when tooled.

4. Set out your gouges and pallets and by trial and error fit the tools to the lines of your drawings – you will soon be able to judge which tool will fit where. When the correct tool has been found, make a firm blind impression on the drawing and write by the side of it which number tool you have used (all gouges and pallets have a tiny number, or sometimes a number and a letter, on their shanks). Gradually a working drawing will emerge.

When working with gouges and pallets the basic rules of tooling apply. Avoid joining them edge to edge, but let them flow into each other by starting the new gouge mark well inside the previous one (Fig 119). This is possible even when a different curve or a change of direction is required. When tooling, do not be afraid to turn your work around – headstands are unnecessary! Always use gouges with the curve opening away from you so you are looking down the shaft to the open face, and keep the tool parallel to your body. Again, practise first before attempting the real thing.

5. Tape the foil in position, making sure it is wrinkle-free, then tape your numbered working drawing in place and tool through this on to your book.

Fig 118   Gouges joined edge to edge.

Fig 119   Gouges correctly joined.

Fig 120   The open face of a gouge.

RAISED DESIGNS

Effective designs and patterns can be made on cloth books using manila, cut, shaped and overlayed to the required design. There are limitations caused by the stretch of the cloth, and additional thicknesses of a relief design should be accounted for in the size of the joint or by using a slightly thinner board.

11   Book Repairs

The bookbinder can easily incorporate parts of an old cover into a new case, but you will find that not all books need to be completely rebound. It is quite possible to carry out simple repairs at home, once you have a good understanding of how a book is constructed and the techniques involved. When repairing, your aim should be to produce a book which is once more strong and useable, yet which retains as much of its original look and feel as possible.

RE-BACKING

The joints or hinges are the parts of the case which take the most punishment. The cloth here often becomes worn and frayed, and it is not uncommon for the spine piece to come away entirely. It is not always necessary to re-case the book, and a neat repair can be accomplished – this is known as re-backing.

We will assume that the book to be repaired has two covered boards and a loose spine piece. The endpapers are split and the sewing and condition of the tapes need attention.
1.   Prepare the work surface.
2.   Collate.
3.   Remove the old spine piece – care is needed here, as old cloth is sometimes fragile. Do not attempt to remove any backing paper at this stage, as it will help to keep the cloth together while you are working on the book.
4.   Most commercially-produced cased bindings have tipped-on endpapers, that is, one folded sheet of paper (sometimes coloured) is 'tipped on' to the first and last sections of the book. We will assume that the joint is weak and in need of strengthening. Carefully ease the free endpapers off the book, if necessary breaking what remains of their attachment to the board papers. Mark them 'front' and 'back' and place them to one side.

Tools	Equipment	Materials
Scalpel, with an old clean No. 10 blade as well as a new one	Pressing boards Lying press Weight Nipping press	Tapes Thin thread Paste and glue Paper to match the endpapers in weight, colour and texture
Bone folder Glue and paste brushes Needle		Cloth to match the book cloth (spines often fade to a completely different colour from the rest of the book, and it is this that your cloth should match)

5. Remove the old boards. As the sewing will be strengthened and the spine lining replaced treat the book as a normal case book, and open the front board and cut through the mull and tapes. Repeat at the back.

6. With the book between rough boards, clean off the old spine linings and the old glue. This is particularly important as most older books were glued with hot animal glue and PVA will not mix with this. If necessary, paste the spine as described on pages 69–70.

7. Strengthen the sewing. Provided the original tapes and sewing are intact, the sewing can be strengthened as follows:

(i) Select tapes as near to the originals in width as possible. Cut the appropriate number, the width of the rounded spine plus 2in (5cm).

(ii) Lightly glue each tape in position over an existing tape.

(iii) Remove the book from the press and place it between rough boards on your bench with the spine towards you.

(iv) You are going to re-sew the first three sections and the last three, and every fourth to sixth section in between. Find the middle of these sections and mark them with little strips of paper.

(v) Using a thin thread, open the topmost section and sew as normal, making sure you use the original sewing holes. Open and sew the second and third sections, tying the two loose ends and forming a kettle stitch as usual. Sew every marked section until the last three which are sewn normally. When you get to the middle of the book you will find it easier, particularly if the book is a heavy one, to turn the book over.

(vi) Some early cased books were sewn on very thin sunken cords. These too can be strengthened using thin tapes, placed with one edge to the sunken cord so that as few extra holes are made in the spine as possible.

8. Replace the book in the press and glue and line the spine with mull and Kraft paper as normal. If the book had a stuck-on head band, this should be replaced before the Kraft paper is put on.

9. Make new paper joints for endpapers.

(i) Cut two strips from matching paper, the length of the original endpaper by 1in (2.5cm). A slightly rough edge is preferable to a hard cut edge, so tear the paper against your straight edge rather than cutting it.

(ii) Lay the first free endpaper (or fly leaf) coloured side down on a sheet of clean waste.

(iii) With a folded sheet of waste, mask all but $\frac{1}{8}$in (2.5mm) at the spine edge of the endpaper. Paste this strip.

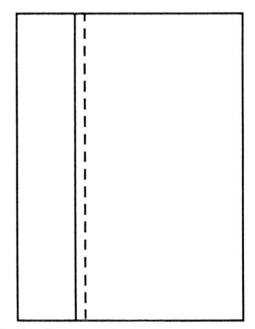

Fig 121   Pasting an extension to an existing endpaper.

(iv)   With the coloured side down, place one strip to the pasted $\frac{1}{8}$ so that the remaining $\frac{7}{8}$ of the strip protrudes from the spine edge, providing an extension to the free endpaper. Using a bone folder make sure that both pasted edges are well stuck down. Placing the paper between terylene, waste sheets and pressing boards, nip, and then allow to dry. Trim off excess at the head and tail. Repeat with the second endpaper.

10.   When the endpapers are dry they can be reattached to the book. As the book will have been rounded and backed, your new endpaper must be made to fit into the joint.

(i)   Measure the joint of the book with dividers.

(ii)   Fold over the new extension of your repaired endpaper where the original fold would have been, colour to colour. From the fold, mark the depth of the joint.

(iii)   Placing your metal straight edge along the joint line, work the fold along the edge of your straight edge with a bone folder, thus forming the joint.

(iv)   Tip each endpaper into position.

11.   Prepare the case as follows:

(i)   Lift the board cloth to a depth of 1in (2.5cm) from the spine edge of both boards – this is best accomplished with a not too sharp rounded blade, such as a No. 10 scalpel blade. A sharp blade could easily cut the cloth, whereas an old blade will be fine enough to wriggle underneath the cloth without damaging it. When you reach the turn-ins slit the cloth along the board edge, again to the depth of 1in (2.5cm). When the board cloth is free, insert your straight edge lengthways between the cloth and the board, and ease it open. Avoid actually creasing the cloth.

(ii)   Turn the board over and lift the spine edge of the pasted-down endpaper, again to a depth of 1in (2.5cm). Start with the cloth turn-in and work your way along, lifting the mull with the paper as this will strengthen it. When you have lifted the strip, open it with your straight edge. The mull, and possibly a thin layer of board, should peel off easily. Start by lifting an inside corner and carefully pull along, but towards, the cut edge.

(iii)   Trimming the board cloth is a matter of judgement. If the edge is very badly frayed, a little neatening is acceptable. If the case has a decorative line close to the joint, trimming the cloth just outside this line can help to camouflage the repair. If you have to trim the cloth considerably, a thin manila strip glued between the edge of the cloth and the board edge will avoid unsightly and vulnerable cloth edges.

Fig 122   A thin manila strip in place.

(iv)   If the spine piece has been damaged a thin manila frame can be made for the spine to fit in. This is then glued to the manila spine stiffener. Cut two spine stiffeners, the length of the boards by the width of the rounded spine. Place the old spine, trimmed and neatened as necessary, in position on one piece of manila. Draw around the spine piece, using a needle or pencil, and, with a No. 10A scalpel blade, cut out the silhouette. Glue the frame to the second manila and mark the head.

12.   Cut the cloth strip, the length of the boards plus the length of two of the book's turn-ins (not less than ½in (1cm) each), by the width of the rounded spine plus two joint widths (as for normal case binding) plus 2in (5cm). The only difference may be with the size of the joint. Many older books do not have a French groove, and instead you may find that a slightly thinner board was used and that this was placed up to the joint. If this is the case with your book then the joint allowance must be correspondingly reduced to ⅛in (2.5mm).

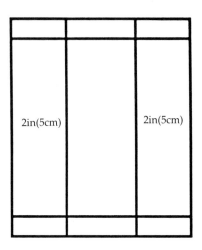

Fig 123   A cloth spine strip with measurements.

13.   Glue your cloth and place the manila spine stiffener in position. Rub down with a bone folder.

14.   Holding the old board cloth back, place the boards in position. Before you turn in the cloth at the head and tail, check that your case fits by placing the book in it. If it is too tight or too big when closed, adjust the boards accordingly. Turn in at the head and tail.

15.   With waste paper beneath, clean off any old board from the underside of the cloth before glueing it back in position.

16.   Glue the old cloth turn-ins and re-position. Rub down firmly and allow to dry.

17.   Case the book. Treat the new endpaper flange as though you were pasting down a complete endpaper for a cased book.

(i)   Place a piece of waste between the flange, mull and tapes, and paste.

(ii)   Holding the old board paper flap out of the way, position the book. Paste the second flange, mull and tapes.

(iii)   Wrap the case around the book, and with waste sheets inside and outside, nip.

(iv)   Paste the board paper flanges and put down over the new paper. Nip.

18.   Dry under a light weight.

19.   Remove any traces from the old spine piece of old spine linings, using paste to dampen old adhesives if necessary. Glue spine piece in position, rub down firmly.

You may find that if animal glue was used on the original cloth paste works better for sticking than PVA. Frayed board edges can be strengthened by rubbing a little paste along them.

CORNERS

Damaged corners can be strengthened and repaired, and if a corner is missing it is possible to rebuild it.

Tools	Materials
Scalpel	Paste
Hammer	Grey-board
Paste brush	Cloth
Knocking down iron	
Bone folder	

1. Lift the old cloth away from the corner, and slit it along the edge of the board, but only as far as is strictly necessary. Lift the endpaper and turn-ins.
2. Separate the old board at the corner into layers, inserting the blade of your knife to a depth of $\frac{1}{8}$ to $\frac{1}{4}$in (2.5–5mm).

3. Taking a small piece of grey-board, peel off a thin layer, preferably from one corner, slightly larger than you will need for replacing the corner. With a sharp blade, bevel the rough edge. Repeat until you have a small pile of pieces.
4. Paste inside the lower layer of your old board, insert the thinnest edge of a grey-board piece and in this way gradually build up the corner.
5. Place the built-up corner on your knocking down iron, held securely at one end of the lying press, and protect it with a piece of waste paper. The best sort of paper for this is a silicone-release paper, as the pasted corner will not stick to it. With another piece of protective waste on top of the corner, gently tap it with a hammer, closing the layers and consolidating the corner.
6. Allow the corner to dry and then trim

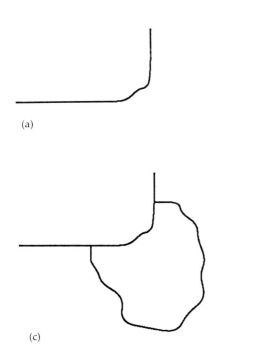

(a)

(c)

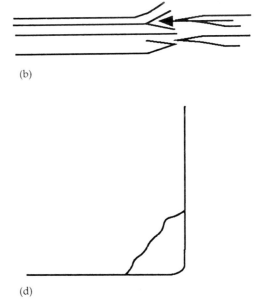

(b)

(d)

Fig 124   (a), (b), (c) and (d) Building up a corner.

off any excess board with a knife and straight edge. If the book is elderly, sandpaper the corner so that it does not look too aggressively sharp.

Recovering Damaged Corners

Even if your corners do not need replacing, very often the old cloth will have become worn and the board will be showing. The method of dealing with this is as follows:

1. Lift the endpaper at the corner, and the cloth on the board and turn-ins. The amount of cloth you lift will depend, as always, upon the size of the book and the extent of the damage, but usually a depth of $\frac{1}{2}-\frac{3}{4}$in (10–15mm) will suffice. Ensure that any exposed board will be covered by the new cloth.
2. Cut paper templates for each corner, allowing at least $\frac{1}{2}$in (1cm) turn-in.
3. Cut out your cloth corners, and mark the turn-ins.
4. Glue and position the corners one at a time on the book, keeping the old cloth clear and clean. As before, mitre the corners, allowing a depth of one board thickness plus $\frac{1}{32}$in (0.6mm). Turn in the corners.
5. A gentle tap with a hammer, again with the corner on a firm surface or knocking down iron, can help when you are working with older books whose corners have become a little tired and have started to turn inwards. Glue and position the old cloth and turn-ins. Rub a little paste along the board edges for strength.

I have described how to repair an average cloth-cased book, but you must remember that each book is different. Examine your book carefully before you decide to take it apart. Occasionally you may come across a rare or valuable book which as an amateur you should not tackle – you will probably do more harm than good. These books should be left alone and, if necessary, a protective box should be made for them to live in.

12 Paper Repairs

OLD ENDPAPERS

Occasionally you will want to retain the old endpapers of a book. There is more than one way of tackling this.

Dry Method

If the old boards are not to be re-used the following method should be adopted.

1. Remove the book from its case. If the endpapers are intact, carefully lift the coloured free paper off the book so that the old mull and tapes are exposed. This will enable you to cut through them without damaging the endpaper. Remove the old cloth from the case.
2. Do not try to lift the paste-down from the board. Instead, remove the board from the paste-down endpaper. Working on a flat hard surface, carefully peel off strips of board until the reverse side of the paste-down is revealed. The last layers of board can be removed by applying some thin paste, leaving for about 10 minutes and then scraping off.
3. Strengthen the fold of the endpapers with Kozushi.

Wet Method

Alternatively, the endpaper can be soaked off. Before attempting this method, you must check that the printing inks are stable in water by dropping a tiny amount of water on to an unobtrusive part of the paper. Leave for a few minutes and then observe any bleeding of the ink – this is best done through a magnifying glass. If the ink runs at all then the wet method is unsuitable.

1. Using clean water and cotton wool, thoroughly wet the whole paste-down. Gradually the water will penetrate the paper and dissolve the paste or glue underneath. Avoid the temptation to fiddle with the corner of the paper before it is ready as this could stretch or even tear the paper.
2. When the adhesive has softened thoroughly, the paste-down should lift off easily. Remember that wet paper is fragile and should be handled with care.
3. Another method is to remove the cloth and simply place the endpaper and board in a bath of cold water, allowing the endpaper to float off.
4. If the endpapers have split, as before, paste a 1in (2.5cm) wide extension to the free endpaper, put down as before and paste the paste-down in after the book has been cased.

CLEANING

Although washing a whole book is not recommended for the amateur binder, individual soiled pages can be cleaned at home.

Dry Cleaning Methods

A Soft Brush

Much surface dirt and mould can be removed by gently brushing away from you with a soft, thick brush. This method is particularly useful for cleaning out the dirt that frequently nestles in the folds of sections.

Rubbing

Powdered art gum or draft cleaning powder is probably the best and easiest way of dealing with ingrained dirt. Sprinkle a little powder on the surface to be cleaned and gently rub in circles with the tips of your fingers, a small area at a time. As the powder becomes soiled, brush it away and continue until no more dirt will come off. Great care must be taken to ensure the soundness of the paper as brittle paper could easily be damaged by too energetic cleansing.

Washing

Washing paper in water will remove water-soluble stains, reduce water stains and also flatten out wrinkles and other distortions. Before washing, the following points must be considered:

● Water will actually set surface dust, so the paper should be dry-cleaned first
● Gelatine sizing in paper will be reduced
● If the paper is fragile it is unwise to attempt washing
● Inks and coloureds must be tested for solubility
● Coated papers can lose their coating when wet and should not be washed

However, if you are determined . . .

1. Test the inks for solubility. Dampen a small wad of cotton wool $\frac{1}{4}$ to $\frac{1}{2}$in (5–10mm) in diameter, squeeze out any excess water and place it on an insignificant part of the text to be washed. Leave it for about 3 minutes, then remove it and examine the moistened area through a magnifying glass for any signs of feathering, bleeding or discolouration. The cotton wool should also be examined.
2. A second test is to dampen a small portion of the text by lightly brushing it with a thin wet brush. Again signs of damage can then be looked for.

Provided the paper is sound, and the ink insoluble, you should be able to wash your soiled page. Beware, however, of washing heavily-textured paper or engravings, or etchings where the plate marks are visible – these should be preserved and can be removed by washing.

Equipment	Materials
Small tray, about 2in (5cm) deep and large enough to hold the page to be washed – a photographic tray is ideal	Polyester fabric or wet strength paper
Soft brush	Absorbent paper, such as heavy blotting paper
Treble washing line to dry the paper (Fig 125)	

1. Fill the tray with cold (preferably distilled) water.
2. Support the page to be washed on a piece of polyester or wet strength paper.
3. Immerse in the water, lowering the paper on its support into the bath from the middle (Fig 126).
4. Gently move the water so that the page is immersed but not duly disturbed.

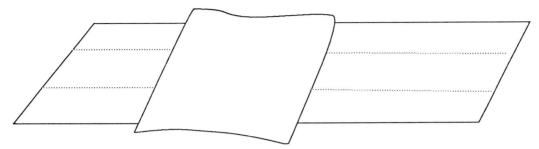

Fig 125   Washing lines.

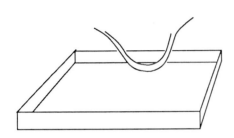

Fig 126   Lowering a piece of paper on its support into the bath.

Leave in the bath for about 15 minutes, occasionally moving the water.

5.   Lift the paper from the bath using the support material.

6.   Place a sheet of absorbent paper on the line and lay the washed paper on it to dry, having first blotted off any excess water. Replace the absorbent paper as necessary.

RE-SIZING

Should your paper have lost much of its original size while being washed, it will be necessary to re-size it. For most cloth-cased books a nylon size made from soluble nylon powder (Calaton) dissolved in industrial methylated spirits or isopropyl alcohol can be used. Ask your chemist to make you up a 5 per cent solution which can be brushed on to the paper. You may find that the size thickens during storage, and if this is the case, you should stand it in a basin of warm water until it liquefies. For better quality paper a warm gelatine size should be used. This can be made by dissolving 2oz (50g) gelatine size, again available from your chemist, in 8 pints (3.5 litres) of warm water. After washing, the paper is immersed in a bath of the warm size for 10 to 15 minutes, excess size is blotted off and then the paper is dried as before. It is advisable to separate the paper from the blotting paper with a piece of polyester fabric.

PAPER TEARS

Crompton tissue is a thin tissue backed with a heat-sensitive adhesive which is very useful for small repairs, and particularly for repairing tears without taking the book apart. The tissue is backed with a release paper, which also has many other uses in the bindery.

1.   Cut a manageable piece of Crompton tissue with its backing.

2.   Place the paper with the edges of the tear together, so that they overlap correctly, on your light box (Fig 127).

129

Tools	Equipment	Materials
Needle	Polishing iron	Crompton tissue
Scissors	Finishing stove, or household iron	Acetate or heavy clear plastic sheet
	Light box – made by resting a sheet of plate glass about 24 × 16in (60 × 40cm) on 4 bricks with a small light underneath (Fig 128)	

3. Put a protective sheet of clean acetate over the tear.

4. Switch on the light. The tear should be easily seen.

5. Remove a small piece of Crompton tissue from its backing and place it over the tear.

6. With your needle, mark out your repair tissue, following the shape of the tear, so that you have a strip about ¼in (5mm) wide and slightly longer than the tear. *Tear* your strip out – the slightly rough edges will blend with the paper.

7. Turn the paper over and mark out a similar repair for the reverse. (For tiny tears this will not be necessary.)

8. Remove the page from the light box.

9. Check that the edges of the tear are together as before.

10. With a warm polishing iron, or if you do not possess this, a warm domestic iron, lightly tack the repair tissue in place.

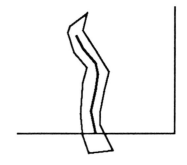

Fig 127 Repair tissue in place.

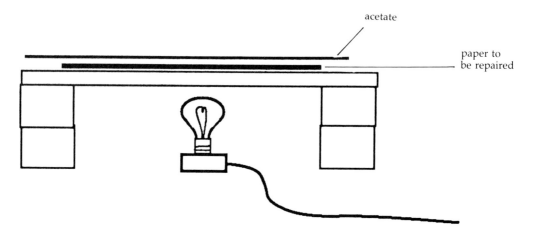

Fig 128 Home-made light box.

The adhesive side, which is the shinier of the two, should be next to the paper. Always iron through release paper, never directly on to the page.

11. When the tissue is tacked in place, more heat and pressure can be applied (still through a protective layer of release paper) until the tissue is firmly attached to the paper, when it should be barely visible.

12. Trim off the excess.

Replacing Torn Edges and Lost Corners

1. Place the damaged paper on the light box.

2. Put a protective sheet of acetate over the paper.

3. Switch on the light.

4. Place repair paper over damaged area. As always, the repair paper should be as close to the original in colour, weight and texture as possible. If chain or laid lines are visible on the original page, they should be matched and lined up by the repair paper. When replacing corners and edges, the repair paper should extend beyond the page by $\frac{1}{2}$in (1cm). This will be trimmed later.

5. With your needle draw round the edge of the tear, overlapping it by a slight amount ($\frac{1}{32}$in (0.6mm)).

6. With a damp fine paint brush, draw along the line marked by the needle. This will weaken the paper along the score and make it easier to tear, again giving a slightly rough edge.

Tools	Equipment	Materials
Needle	Polishing iron	Crompton tissue
Scissors	Finishing stove, or	Matching repair paper
Fine paint brush	household iron	Water
	Light box	

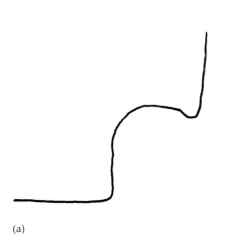

(a)

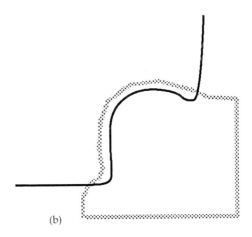

(b)

Fig 129   (a) and (b) Repairing a torn corner.

7.   Remove the acetate sheet and place the repair paper in position. Replace the acetate and place a piece of Crompton tissue over the repair. With a needle, mark the tear line, overlapping it by $\frac{1}{8}$in (2.5mm) and the edge of the page by $\frac{1}{4}$–$\frac{3}{8}$in (5–8mm). Tear the tissue. Repeat on the reverse of the page.

8.   Attach the Crompton tissue as before.

9.   Trim.

STRENGTHENING MAPS AND WHOLE PAGES

Maps and whole pages can be strengthened by a fine Crompton tissue, but you must remember that the tissue is really designed for use with a heat-sealing machine. This is rather like a nipping press with hot plates, and can not only be set to the correct temperature but can also exert considerable pressure. Although a polishing or domestic iron can be used successfully when attaching small areas of repair tissue, it is difficult to maintain the pressure required for a larger area. An alternative to Crompton tissue is to use a fine Japanese tissue or lens tissue. This is pasted over the tear or repair, rubbed down with a bone folder through waste and allowed to dry. By using a fine wet water-colour brush instead of a needle to mark the tear line on your tissue, you will find that the tissue not only tears easily but provides you with a soft fibrous edge.

This will blend better with the paper than a hard cut edge.

Wet Repairs

A more sympathetic repair can be carried out, using either a fine Japanese paper such as Tengujo, or a lens tissue.

This method can be used for replacing torn areas, mending tears, or strengthening and straightening out a damaged sheet. The paper to be repaired should be clean and the ink tested for water solubility before you start. Make sure the glass of your light box is spotless.

1.   Squeeze water from the sponge on to the glass surface of the light box, and sponge down a sheet of polythene on to it, making sure that it is as flat as possible.

2.   Lay the damaged page on to the polythene and dampen it, carefully easing out the creases, so that it is lying flat. Remember not to force the paper. The creases will come out of their own accord once they are wet, and all you should have to do is to nudge the paper carefully into position.

3.   Sponge a second sheet of polythene on top of the damaged page, working out all creases and air bubbles. The paper is now sandwiched.

4.   Place the protective acetate sheet on top of the area to be repaired.

5.   Put repair tissue and repair fill-in paper (if applicable) in turn over the damaged

Tools	Equipment	Materials
Fine brush	Light box	Repair paper
Bone folder	Clear acetate sheet	Water
Needle	3 sheets of thin clear	Japanese tissue
Sponge	polythene	Paste

areas. Mark out the repairs with a needle as described before. Once the repairs have been marked, tear them out.

6. Sponge out a third piece of polythene. Dampen the surface.
7. Turn the repair tissue on to this, using a barely damp sponge, flatten the tissue and remove the excess moisture.
8. Turn back the polythene from the damaged page.
9. Paste the damaged area.
10. Turn the repair tissue on its polythene support over on to the damaged area. Sponge into position and remove the polythene support.
11. Replace the polythene on top of the damaged page and turn over the sandwiched page to reveal the reverse.
12. Remove the uppermost polythene sheet and fill in any missing areas. Paste the whole area to be filled, position the repair and sponge down thoroughly with a barely damp sponge, removing any excess paste as you do so.
13. Repeat 4 to 11 with tissue.
14. Remove the uppermost layer of polythene and turn the page over on to a polyester lining material and absorbent paper. The lining fabric will act as an absorbent buffer between the mended sheet and the absorbent paper, and prevent the two sticking together.
15. Nip and remove from press.
16. Allow to dry, changing the absorbent papers regularly.

This method can also be used most successfully for applying large areas of tissue like Kozushi to the backs of maps and folding-out pages.

REMOVAL OF STICKY TAPE

The removal of sticky tape is a constant problem. Do not try to tear it off as you will damage the paper. The best solvent is benzene, which is available from good chemists. This must be used according to the following rules:

- Always use in a well-ventilated room
- Avoid contact with the skin
- Apply with a cotton wool swab, wrapped around a wooden cocktail stick or pencil, or with a soft flat paint brush

Method

1. Apply the benzene to the reverse side of the page with sticky tape on it.
2. As the solvent softens the adhesive, lift the tape with a pair of tweezers.
3. Remove any remaining adhesive by applying the solvent and immediately wiping away the residue with cotton wool.

If the sticky tape is on both sides of the paper, apply the solvent with a brush to a corner of the tape. Again lift with tweezers, continually applying the solvent and lifting the tape as the adhesive softens.

13 Projects

SLIP CASE

Slip cases are used to provide some protection for books. They are not as satisfactory as boxes, as the spine of the book is left exposed; there is also the risk of damage being done as the book is slid in and out of the case, rather than being lifted out of a box. However, they have their uses and this project will serve as an introduction to box making.

Tools	Materials
Glue brush	Board
Knife	Glue
Straight edge	Cloth
6in (15cm) length of	Manila
1in (2.5cm)	Lining material – felt
dowelling (an old	
broom handle is	
ideal)	
Fine sandpaper	

When working out the measurements for boxes, work from the materials, making up little jigs of the required thicknesses.

1. Cut 2 side pieces, 1 head and 1 tail piece, and 1 spine piece of board. These boards are cut using exactly the same cutting methods as the book boards. First of all, cut two pieces of square board with the grain running from head to tail, making the board 1in (2.5cm) longer and $\frac{1}{2}$in (1cm) wider than the book. Cut them accurately to size. When measuring the board thicknesses and linings, do not squash the felt as its true thickness must be measured.
2. Thumb-holes on the foredges of the slip case can make removing the book easier (but are not essential).
(i) Tack the two side boards accurately together with either double-sided masking tape or tiny dabs of glue.

Measurements

Side pieces (2)   Height = height of book boards + 2 thicknesses of board + 2 linings
Width = width of book measured from the round to the foredge + 1 thickness of board + 1 lining

Head and tail pieces   Length = width of spine pieces
Width = width of book, measured from the widest point + 2 linings

Spine piece   Length = length of book + 2 linings
Width equals width of book + 2 linings

(ii) Mark a semicircle on the foredges, about 1in (2.5cm) wide and ½in (1cm) deep (a 10p piece is a useful guide) slightly up from the central line.

(iii) With the two boards firmly together, roughly cut out the semicircle with a strong sharp blade, being careful not to overlap the outlines.

(iv) Wrap a strip of fine sandpaper around your strip of dowelling and finish off the thumb-hole by working the sander backwards and forwards until it is smooth.

Release the boards, sand off any roughness caused where the boards were tacked together. This method ensures that the thumb-holes will be smooth and exactly in alignment.

3. Line the boards.

(i) The side boards. Leave one board thickness from the edge at the head, tail and spine and ¼in (5mm) from the edge at the foredge. If you have made a thumb-hole, do not forget to follow the edge of this. Make a paper template for the felt before cutting it out and glueing it to the board, leaving ¾in (15mm) unstuck on the foredge to allow the covering material to be turned in. You may find it easier to glue the board and stick the felt to it rather than the other way round.

(ii) Head and tail pieces. Line to the edges of these but allow ¼in (5mm) border along the foredge and leave ¾in (15mm) unstuck.

(iii) Spine piece. This is completely lined.

4. Making up the slip case.

(i) Glue one long edge and the spine edge of the head piece; glue this in position on one of the side boards.

(ii) Glue one long edge and the head edge of the spine piece and position.

(iii) Glue and position the tail piece.

(iv) Finally, glue the three exposed long edges of the sides and place the second side board in position. Place weights at the corners and allow to dry.

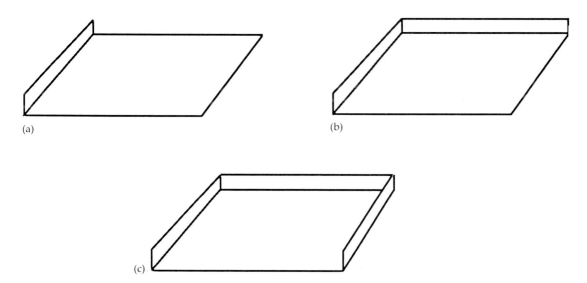

(a)

(b)

(c)

Fig 130   (a), (b) and (c) Glueing and positioning the slip-case boards.

(v) You will have exposed edges of board along the head, tail and spine. Cut manila strips the exact width and length of all three sides, glue into position and rub down firmly. Allow to dry for at least 1 hour.

(vi) When the manila is dry, sand the edges with a piece of sandpaper strapped around your metal straight edge or a wooden block.

(vii) Mark out and cut the cloth. Lay the slip case on its side on the cloth. Draw around the side. Turn the case on to its spine, mark, then turn the case over on to its second side and mark. Allow ½in (1cm) turn-in on the foredges, and ¼in (5mm) turn-in at the head and tail (Fig 131).

5. Glue one side of the case and place it in position on the cloth. Rub the cloth down firmly. Glue the spine, wrap the cloth over and rub down. Glue the second board, bring the cloth over again, and rub down firmly.

6. Turn in the cloth at the head and tail.

(i) Stand the case on its spine.

(ii) Slit the cloth along the fold of the turn-in at all four corners.

(iii) Mitre the corners to 45°, $\frac{1}{32}$in (0.6mm) away from the board.

7. To avoid excess bulk on the foredge fold the cloth at the head, and then stand the case on its head. You will see that if

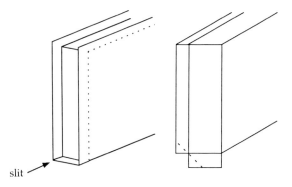

Fig 132　Slit cloth along fold of turn-in, and then mitre the corners to 45 degrees.

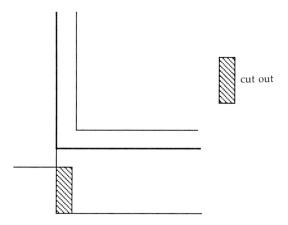

Fig 133　Avoiding excess bulk on the foredge.

you try to turn the cloth in at the sides and foredge without cutting it, there is a lot of excess cloth in the corner. To avoid this problem, cut out a strip of cloth one board thickness wide from the fold of the cloth and leaving one board thickness of cloth on the foredge. Do this at all four corners.

8. Glue and turn in the cloth along the head and tail of the slip case.

9. Turn in the cloth along the foredges, making sure that the corners are as neat as possible, and that the cloth goes inside the lining material.

10. If you have made thumb-holes, you will find that the cloth will not stretch round them, and that a series of cuts must

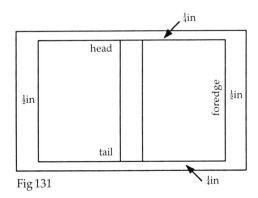

Fig 131

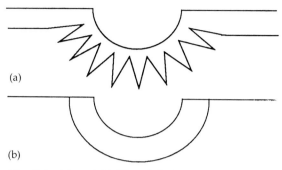
(a)

(b)

Fig 134 (a) and (b) Thumb-holes.

be made on the inside to enable the cloth to travel round the curve.
11. Cut two semicircular pieces of cloth to cover the cuts. Glue them in position.
12. Cover the head and tail. With heavy paper (cartridge), fill in the space between the turnings at the head and tail. Cut two pieces of cloth $\frac{1}{16}$in (1.25mm) less than the width of the head and tail by the length plus $\frac{1}{2}$in (1cm). Glue the cloths in position,

turning them in at the foredge. A little trimming at the corners of the turn-in will help to avoid more bulk at the corners.
10. Glue down the linings.
11. Allow to dry.

SIMPLE DROP-BACK BOX

A box is a much more satisfactory place to keep a book safe than a slip case. Not only is the whole book protected, but there is less risk of damage to the book when it is being removed.

Tools	Materials
Knife	Board
Glue brush	Glue
Straight edge	Cloth
Scissors	Manila
Bone folder	Lining felt

Measurements

Base   Length = length of book + 2 board thicknesses + 2 linings
          Width = width of book + 1 board thickness + 1 lining

Base   Long back wall: Length = length of base
                    Height = thickness of book + 1 lining
          Short side walls: Length = width of base *minus* 1 board thickness
                   Height = height of back wall

Lid   Length = length of book + 2 linings + 4 board thicknesses + 4 cloth
        thicknesses + 2 manila thicknesses + $\frac{1}{16}$in (1.25mm)
        Width = width of book + 1 lining + 2 board thicknesses + 2 cloth thicknesses
        + 1 manila + $\frac{1}{32}$in (0.6mm).

Lid walls   Long side wall: Length = length of lid
                    Height = thickness of book + 2 linings + 1 board
        thickness
        Short side walls: Length = width of the lid *minus* 1 board thickness
                 Height = height of long side wall

Spine piece   Length = length of lid
          Height = height of lid sides + 1 board thickness

1. Cut boards – 1 lid and 3 walls; 1 base and 3 walls; and 1 spine piece. Measurements must be accurate. The width of the book is measured from the rounded spine to the foredge of the board. The thickness is measured from the thickest part of the book, which is usually the middle.

2. Assemble the two trays – the base (glue and position the walls), and the lid (glue and position the walls). Allow to dry. To help adhesion, weights can be placed across the corners.

3. When dry, glue manila strips (cut to size) to the outside of the wall to cover and strengthen the joins. Dry, then sandpaper so that all the edges are smooth.

4. Test that the lid fits comfortably over the base.

5. Line the inner ends of the walls with cloth.

(i) Cut out four strips of cloth, $\frac{1}{2}$–$\frac{5}{8}$in (10–12.5mm) wide by the height of the wall plus one thickness of board plus $\frac{1}{2}$in (10mm).

(ii) Mark the four strips (*see* Fig 135).

(iii) Cut off mitre.

(iv) Cut along the line at the base to a depth of 1 board thickness. Remember that the head and tail strips will be the reverse of each other.

(v) Glue the cloth to the edge of the board. Wrap the cloth around the board inside and outside. Turn over the cloth at the head, working the corners neatly, following the sequence numbered on Fig 136.

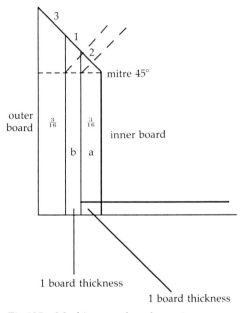

Fig 135 Marking out the edge strip.

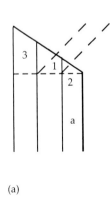

(a)

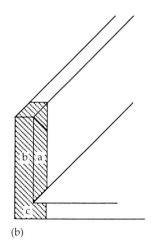

(b)

Fig 136 (a) and (b) Sequences for covering the foredge.

6. Mark and cut out the covering cloth.
(i)   Lay the lid on the cloth. Allow a margin of at least 2½ times the height of the walls from the edge of the cloth, and draw one long pitching line from the head for the lid and spine. Draw around the lid base.
(ii)   Keeping the edge of the lid base on the guide lines, tip the tray over – first on to its head, then on to its tail, then back – drawing around each. As the flaps of the lid cover the inside of the walls as well, the cloth should be twice the height of the walls. Add 1 wall height to each flap plus ½in (1cm).
(iii)   Lay the spine piece in position, leaving a gap of 1 board thickness plus 2 thicknesses of cloth between the spine piece and the base and the spine piece and the lid. Place the base in position. As it is smaller than the lid it is pitched 1 board thickness plus 1 manilla plus 1 cloth thickness inside the pitching line. Draw around the base.
(iv)   The walls of the base are marked out in the same way as the lid, but the cloth is

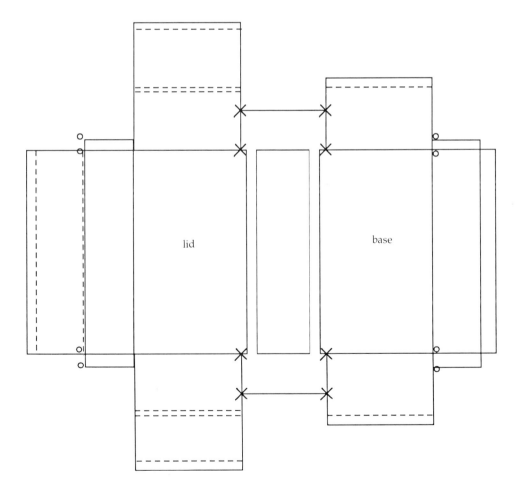

Fig 137   Cloth marked out for the box.

not turned in to cover the whole of the inside wall. The flaps therefore should be the height of the walls plus ½in (1cm).

7. Mark out the cloth. On your cloth to each back piece add a side turn-in flap, ½in (1cm) wide by the height of the wall.

8. (i) Glue the base of the lid and position it on the cloth. Turn it over, supporting the tray on a pile of backing boards, and rub the cloth down firmly. Repeat with the base.

(ii) Glue the spine piece in position.

(iii) With a knife and straight edge cut the following points, marked on Fig 138 – X to X, ⅛in (2.5mm) in from the spine edge. Trim off excess length to 1in (2.5cm). To facilitate the turn-in, cut out a notch 1 board thickness wide by ⅛in (2.5mm) from the base of the lid side of the spine flap and 2 board thicknesses wide from the base of the base side spine flap. Glue and turn the cloth over the edge of the spine piece, travelling around the ends of the side walls with your notches.

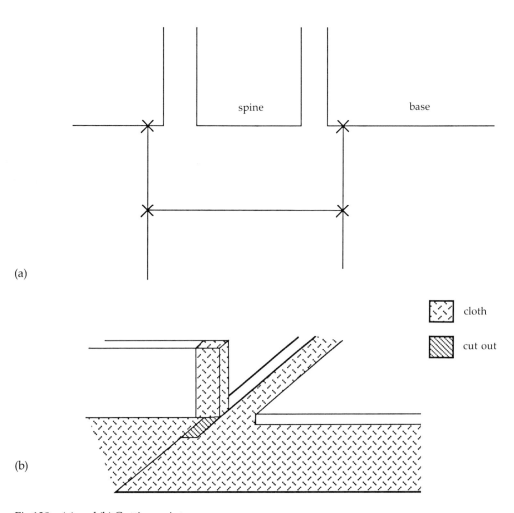

(a)

(b)

cloth

cut out

Fig 138   (a) and (b) Cutting points.

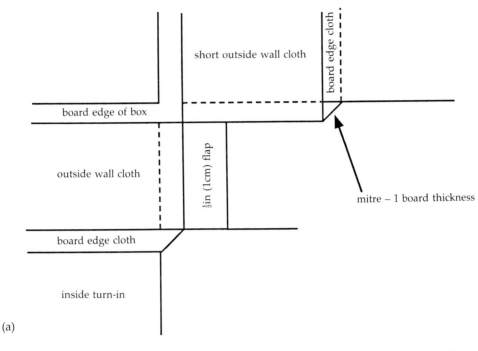

short outside wall cloth

board edge cloth

board edge of box

outside wall cloth

½in (1cm) flap

mitre – 1 board thickness

board edge cloth

inside turn-in

(a)

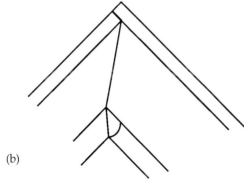

(b)

Fig 139 (a) and (b) Cutting cloth for the corners.

(iv) Slit along the back wall flaps 0 to 0 (*see* Fig 137).

(v) At the corners, draw and cut a 45° mitre the same length as the thickness of the board. Trim off 1 board thickness from the turn-in cloth. Trim, mitre and trim the inside of the short walls in the same way.

(vi) Glue the back strips of the base in position and rub down. Glue down corner flaps and turn-ins.

(vii) Glue and rub down the side pieces.

(viii) Repeat with the lid, glueing the cloth down firmly to the inside boards. Mitre the corners of the cloth and remove the excess from the bottom of the lid by placing your 45° set square against the wall and cutting away the cloth with a scalpel.

9. Line the spine of the box with cloth.

(i) Cut a strip of cloth the length of the inside of the longest tray by the width of the spine plus the width allowed for the hinge plus 2in (5cm). The cloth is to over-lap each board by 1in (2.5cm) so that it fits around the walls of the smaller base tray.

(ii) Rule a line 1in (2.5cm) from the long edge of the strip. At the head and tail of this line, trim off a strip 1 board thickness wide.

(iii) Glue the cloth and stick to the base tray. Work along the hinge, over the spine, along the second hinge and on to the lid.

141

Fig 140 Drop-back box for single-section magazines.

10. Cut out the lining felt – it should cover the three walls, the floor of the base and the floor of the lid only. (It is sometimes easier to cut felt if it is sandwiched between two pieces of thin card and cut with a sharp knife and straight edge.) Glue the felt in position and allow it to dry.

A piece of felt can be glued to the spine piece, the length of the inside of the base tray by the inside board height, but in this case one felt thickness must be added to the width of both trays when you begin.

142

FOLDER OR PORTFOLIO

Tools	Materials
Bone folder	Board
Knife	Decorative covering
Set square	paper
Scissors	½in (1cm) tape or
Hammer	ribbon
Straight edge	Cloth
Glue brush	Glue
	Plain lining paper

No large pieces of equipment, other than a solid smooth working surface, are needed for this. The measurements I have given are for making a folder to carry an A3 sketch book. You can make your folder smaller or larger, as you wish.
1.   Cut the boards – 2 boards A3 length + ½in (1cm), by A3 width + ½in (1cm); 2 short side pieces, the width of the main board by 4in (10cm); 1 long side piece, the length of the main board by 4in (10cm).

2.   Cut a strip of cloth for the centre covering material 7in (17.5cm) wide by the length of the board + 2in (5cm) (to allow 1in (2.5cm) turn-in at the head and tail).
3.   On the reverse side of the cloth mark the 1in (2.5cm) turn-in at the head and tail.
4.   Mark two lines 2in (5cm) in from each edge, leaving a 3in (7.5cm) strip in the middle.
5.   Glue the cloth. Place the boards in position up to the 2in (5cm) line and rub down. Turn in the cloth at the head and tail.
6.   Mitre two corners of each side piece.
(i)   Set your dividers to 1in (2.5cm). Mark 1in (2.5cm) along each side from the corners.
(ii)   Cut along the line with a knife and straight edge.
7.   Cut the material for the side pieces, 7in (17.5cm) wide by the length of the boards + 2in (5cm) for turn-ins. Mark out as the spine piece.

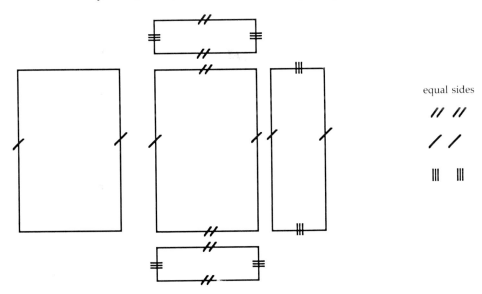

equal sides

Fig 141   Boards for the portfolio.

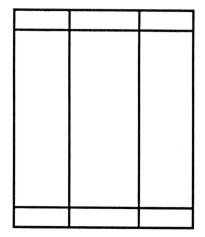

Fig 142   Cloth marked out for the spine piece.

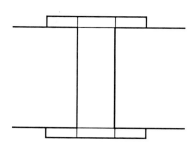

Fig 143   Boards glued in position on the spine piece.

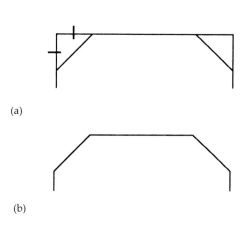

(a)

(b)

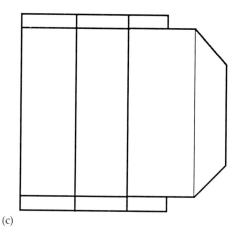

(c)

Fig 144   (a), (b) and (c) Cutting corners for side flaps.

8.   Glue and place the side pieces in pos–ition up to the 2in (5cm) mark. Turn in the sides.

9.   Cover the outside of your large boards with decorative paper, allowing the paper to overlap the cloth by $\frac{1}{16}$in (1.25mm) and again allowing a 1in (2.5cm) turn-in.

10.   On the large boards, make a slit with your knife $\frac{1}{2}$in (1cm) in from the edge, half-way along each outer side, going from the outside to the inside. The slit should be the width of your tape or ribbon plus $\frac{1}{16}$in (1.25mm).

11.   Cut six 9in (22.5cm) tapes. Thread the tapes through the slits, leaving about

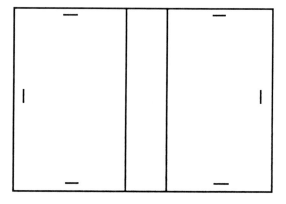

Fig 145   Slits made for the tapes.

144

1in (2.5cm) protruding on the inside. Glue down these spare 1in (2.5cm) ends and hammer into place, to secure them and to close the slit in the board. Remember to hammer through clean waste paper on to a hard firm surface, preferably a knocking down iron held in a lying press.

12.   Cover the remaining areas of the two short and one long side flaps with marbled or decorative paper. Turning the paper round the mitred corners is interesting – a normal 45° mitre will not work, so proceed as follows:

(i)   Allow 1in (2.5cm) turn-in all around.
(ii)   Mark 1 board thickness + $\frac{1}{32}$in (0.6mm) away from the apex of each mitred board corner with a dot.

(iii)   Place the apex of your 90° set square on the dot and mark cutting line ab and ac at each corner. Cut out abc at each corner.
(iv)   Turn in paper along the mitred edge.
(v)   Turn in the paper along the long side, forming a neat corner.
(vi)   Turn in the paper along the short side, forming another neat corner.

13.   Take the long side flap. On the outside of the cloth, mask all but the 2in (5cm) out strip. Glue this 2in (5cm) wide strip to the inside of the long side of one of your large boards.

14.   On the same large board in the same way stick the two short flaps to the inside at the head and tail.

15.   Cut a piece of cloth to line the spine,

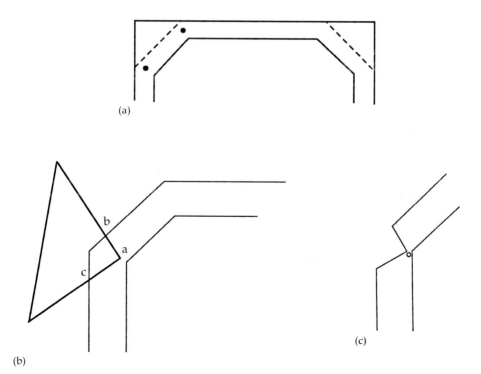

(a)

(b)

(c)

Fig 146   (a), (b) and (c) Covering the side flaps.

145

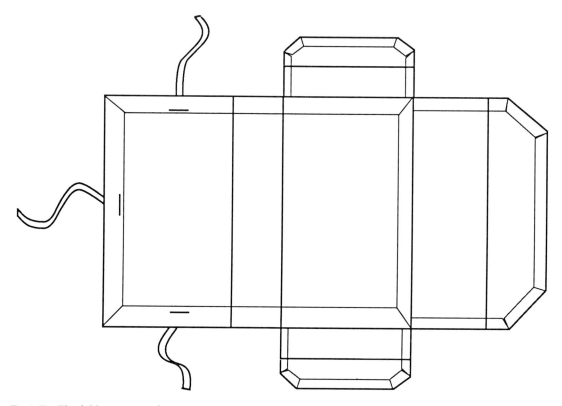

Fig 147   The folder put together.

$\frac{1}{2}$in (1cm) shorter than the length of the spine by 5in (12.5cm) wide. Glue this in position $\frac{1}{4}$in (5mm) from the head and tail, overlapping the inside of each board by 1in (2.5cm).

16.   Similarly, line the inside of the three flaps, cutting the cloth $\frac{1}{2}$in (1cm) less than the length of each flap by 5in (12.5cm) wide.

17.   Cut out and glue a plain lining paper for the two main boards, allowing a border of $\frac{1}{4}$in (5mm).

18.   Cut out and glue lining paper for the three board flaps, again leaving $\frac{1}{4}$in (5mm) border.

19.   Leave to dry.

DESK BLOTTER

Tools	Materials
Bone folder	Thick board
Knife	Decorative paper
Scissors	Thin board or
Glue brush	manila
Straight edge	Cloth
	Glue

You can make this blotter to any size you wish. The best idea is to buy the blotting paper first and then build your blotter neatly around it.

1.   Cut out one piece of thick board $\frac{1}{2}$in

(1cm) longer and $\frac{1}{2}$in (1cm) wider than your blotting paper.

2. Cut one piece of thin board or manila $\frac{1}{4}$in (5mm) longer and $\frac{1}{4}$in (5mm) wider than your blotting paper.

3. Cut out four identical corners in thin board and four in thicker board ($\frac{1}{8}$–$\frac{1}{4}$in (2.5–5mm)) – the thicker ones are to act as fillers for the corners to take up the space needed by the blotting paper. The sizes of the corners will depend upon the size of your blotter. Experiment with different sizes until they look right, using the same principle as when deciding on the size of corner for a half-cloth binding.

4. Cover the large board with cloth, allowing $\frac{3}{4}$in (15mm) turn-in.

5. Cover the smaller thinner board with decorative paper, allowing $\frac{1}{2}$in (1cm) turn-in. To avoid undue stretching of the paper, use glue rather than paste. Nip.

6. Cut the cloth for the corners, allowing a turn-in of $\frac{3}{4}$in (15mm) on the two outer sides, and $\frac{1}{2}$in (1cm) turn-in on the longer third side.

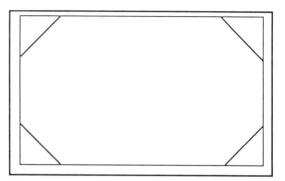

Fig 149   Blotter.

7. Glue the cloth to your thin corner pieces, turning in the cloth along the long third edge only.

8. Tack a thick board filler to the inside of each corner with a small piece of double-sided masking tape.

9. Place one corner in position on the thin board, decorative side up.

10. Turn the board over, keeping the corner piece in position. Mitre the corners, allowing for the thickness of the two thin boards plus the filler plus $\frac{1}{32}$in (0.6mm). It will probably be easiest to glue the appropriate thickness of board together for a jig so that your measurement is accurate.

11. Glue the turn-ins, and turn-in around the thin board so that the corner is now glued to the board by its turn-ins.

12. Repeat 8 to 11 with the other three corners.

13. Glue the thin board with its corners to the exposed board side of the thicker board, leaving $\frac{1}{8}$in (2.5mm) border of cloth all round.

14. When dry, remove the board fillers from the corners.

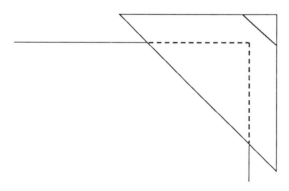

Fig 148   Corners for the blotter.

Appendices

I RECIPES

Flour Paste

4oz (100g) plain flour
1 pint (600ml) water
Few crystals of thymol

1. Add a little cold water to the flour and mix until it forms a smooth paste.
2. Boil the rest of the water and gradually add to the paste, stirring with a wooden spoon. It should start to thicken.
3. Return the mixture to the saucepan (a double saucepan is best) and cook gently for a few minutes.
4. Leave to cool.
5. The addition of two or three drops of thymol is useful as it will help to preserve the paste. Ask your chemist to make up a ten per cent solution of thymol in spirit.

Note: For a stronger paste rice flour can be used.

Gelatine Size

1oz (25g) of parchment or vellum strips to 1 pint (600ml) of water.

1. Put the vellum strips into a double saucepan with the water.
2. Bring to the boil.
3. Simmer for 1 to 1½ hours, until the vellum strips are flabby.
4. Strain the size through muslin. Make up any evaporation loss.

II USING A SEWING FRAME

Sewing on tapes

Although it is perfectly possible to sew on tapes without a sewing frame, particularly with small books, sewing on a frame can make life easier, especially if your book is large.

1. Cut your tapes sufficiently long – to cover the spine of your book, plus 2in (5cm), plus enough tape to reach the bar of the frame and to wrap around it, and also to fit the sewing keys.
2. Wrap the tapes around the specially-designed sewing keys (*see* Fig 150). Pass the keys through the slot in the bed of the frame, positioning them at right angles to the bar.
3. Bring the length of tape up to the bar and wrap it over, pinning it to itself to keep it in position. Try to make the tension as even as possible.
4. Line the tapes up with the tape marks on the spine of your book.
5. Raise the crossbar by tightening the screws until the tapes are taut.
6. Lay the first section on the bed of your frame and sew as usual.

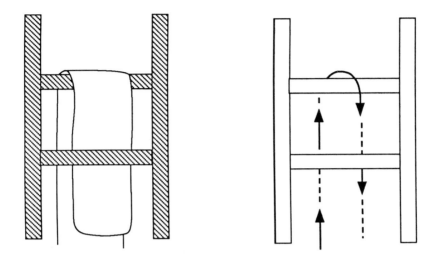

Fig 150   Threading tape into a tape key.

Fig 151   Inserting the tape and key into the slot of the sewing frame.

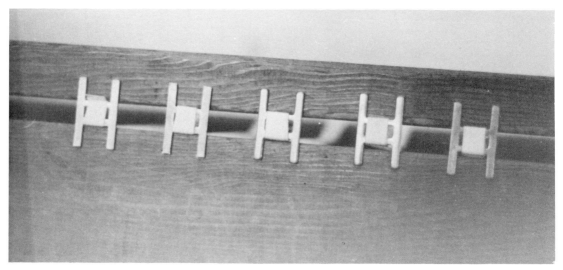

Fig 152   Underside of the sewing frame.

Fig 153   Sewing frame with sewn book.

Glossary

Board paper   The part of the endpaper that is pasted to the board of the book. Sometimes called the pasted-down endpaper, or paste-down.

Cerf   A saw cut made at the head and tail of the book to accommodate the kettle stitches.

Collate   To check that the book is complete and that all the illustrations are present and in the correct order.

Endpapers   Literally, the papers added to the end of the book. They serve as an introduction to the book, leading the reader in as well as being structurally important.

Fillet   A brass wheel used for tooling long lines.

Folio   A single folded sheet of paper consisting of two leaves and four printed sides.

Foredge   The front edge of a book.

French grooves   In modern cased books and library-style bindings the groove that is left between the joint and the front or back board.

Gouges   Curved brass finishing tools.

Guarding   To repair the damaged backs of sections with strips of repair tissue known as guards.

Head   The top of a book, opposite the tail.

Joints   The joint is formed when the book is backed and the sections are hammered over to form the right-angled joints at the spine edges to accommodate the boards. The hinge formed by the covering material on the outside is also referred to as the joint or outer joint.

Kettle stitch   The catch stitch linking the sections together at the head and tail of the book.

Nip   A short sharp press.

Pallets   Straight line finishing tools.

Pulling   Taking the book apart.

Quarto   A section made from a sheet of paper folded twice to give 2 folios, 4 leaves and 8 printed sides.

Reef knot   A knot used for tying two loose ends of thread together at the head or tail of a book. With two loose threads you should note which is behind the other, and tie front over back and then front over back.

Section   Made when a sheet of paper is printed and folded, or just folded. A book is made up of a collection of sections.

Signature   A small letter usually at the foot of the page marking the beginning of each section.

Spine   The back of a book opposite the foredge; also sometimes called the back bone.

Square   The amount of board that projects from the book protecting the leaves.

Swell   Swell is the extra thickness caused in the spine by sewing and guarding.

Tail   The bottom of the book opposite the head.

Tip on   To affix a plate or sheet of paper to another by means of a thin strip of paste (usually $\frac{1}{8}$in); hence the term tipped-on endpapers.

Weaver's knot   A flat, strong knot used to join a new thread to the old one inside a section. Made as follows: 1. With the right end of the thread held behind the left, hold the ends of the two threads in your left hand with about 2in of thread projecting. 2. Wrap the right-hand thread around its own end away from you (clockwise). 3. Wrap the right-hand thread around the left-hand end, still clockwise. 4. Holding the knot firmly in your left hand, take the left end over and through the knot. 5. Pull the right-hand thread only to tighten the knot.

Further Reading

Caring for Books and Documents, A.D. Baynes-Cope (British Museum, 1981)

The Craft of Bookbinding, Eric Burdett (David & Charles, 1975)

Bookbinding and the Care of Books, Douglas Cockerell (Pitman, 1975)

Introduction to Bookbinding, Lionel S. Darley (Faber, 1976)

Bookbinding, Arthur Johnson (Thames and Hudson, 1978)

A History of English Craft – Bookbinding Technique, Bernard Middleton (The Holland Press, 1978)

Introducing Bookbinding, Ivor Robinson (Oxford Polytechnic Press, 1984)

Useful Addresses

Bookcraft Supplies
273 Longhurst Lane
Mellor
Cheshire SK6 5PW
(061 427 7348)
Cloth and other materials, also second-hand tools. Will sell in small quantities.

Archival Aids
PO Box 5
Spondon
Derbyshire DE2 7BD
(0332 666400)
Archival supplies (Crompton tissue, etc).

A.J. Brown Brough & Co. Ltd
3 Dufferin Street
London EC1Y 8SD
(01 638 8085)
Board – bundles only.

Falkiner Fine Papers Ltd
76 Southampton Row
London WC1B 4AR
(01 831 1151)
Paper, also general supplies for book-binding, such as cloth, board, tools and equipment. Minimum order by post £20.00

J. Hewitt & Sons Ltd
3 Prowse Place
London NW1 9PH
(01 485 6252)
General bookbinding supplies – cloth, board, tools and equipment.

P & S Engraving Ltd
38A Norway Street
Portslade
Sussex BN4 1AE
(0273 42480)
Finishing tools.

Papyrus
25 Broad Street
Bath
Avon BA1 5LW
(0225 63418)
Paper.

Russell Bookcrafts
North House
Great North Road
Wyboston
Bedfordshire MK44 3AB
(0480 405464)

George M. Whiley Ltd
Firth Road
Houstoun Industrial Estate
Livingston
West Lothian
Scotland EH54 5DJ
(0506 386115)
Foils and gold leaf.

Index